MY INTERNMENT AND TESTIMONY AT THE NUREMBERG WAR CRIMES TRIAL

My Internment and Testimony at the Nuremberg War Crimes Trial

The Account of Friedrich Rainer, Austrian Nazi

Edited, Annotated, and Introduced by

Maurice Williams

Translated from the German by

Val Witham

The Edwin Mellen Press

Lewiston•Queenston•Lampeter

Library of Congress Cataloging-in-Publication Data

Rainer, Friedrich.
My internment and testimony at the Nuremberg war crimes trial / Friedrich Rainer; edited, annotated, and introduced by Maurice Williams; translated from the German by Val Witham.
p. cm.
Includes bibliographical references and index.

ISBN 0-7734-0803-7

I. Title.

hors série.

A CIP catalog record for this book is available from the British Library.

The Edwin Mellen Press
Box 450
Lewiston, New York
USA 14092-0450

The Edwin Mellen Press
Box 67
Queenston, Ontario
CANADA L0S 1L0

The Edwin Mellen Press, Ltd.
Lampeter, Ceredigion, Wales
UNITED KINGDOM SA48 8LT

Printed in the United States of America

FOR LINDA, DAVID, AND JONATHAN

TABLE OF CONTENTS

PREFACE

During the course of researching a biography of Friedrich Rainer, I discovered the document which is published in this book. Rainer, an Austrian Nazi, a lawyer, the *Gauleiter* and Governor of Carinthia from 1941 to 1945, and a well-connected member of the Hitler hierarchy, was a witness at the main trial of Nazi war criminals in 1945 and 1946. He was detained in the witnesses' wing in Nuremberg from October 1945 until June 1946, an imprisonment which meant he observed firsthand the workings of the International Military Tribunal.

Later, in July 1947, Rainer himself was tried by a Yugoslav military court for crimes against the Slovene people. Found guilty and sentenced to death, he was supposedly executed that same August, and the trial records were closed. Forty-five years later, after the collapse of Tito's Yugoslavia, the declaration of Slovene independence, and the new atmosphere of openness and accessibility, the surviving records of that trial were opened. What emerged were nearly 7000 pages of documents, papers which included much more than his trial records. Rainer had not been immediately executed but worked for his captors writing numerous reports, studies, and analyses, all connected with his Nazi past and involving his German national perspective on the present (i.e., the present of 1947 and 1948). Among those records is this unique account of the Nuremberg trial of the major war criminals, one of the most important pieces which he penned.

Rainer's report, which is located in the Archives of the Republic of Slovenia, is published here in translation in its entirety.

FOREWORD

Today, more than sixty years after the fall of the twelve-year Third Reich, Nazism and particularly its leaders, continue to fascinate the general public around much of the world. How could a high school drop-out from an obscure corner of Austria become the dictator of Germany little more than twelve years after he joined the German Nazi Party? How could he completely tear up the disarmament and territorial provisions of the Treaty of Versailles without firing a shot within six years of his advent to power? How was he able to conquer most of Europe and North Africa only two years after launching the Second World War? Even more fascinating is how this uneducated man could attract such undying devotion from so many educated and intelligent people.

It is tempting to classify the term "intelligent Nazi" as an oxymoron, right alongside my personal favorites: "military intelligence" and "economic expert." And yet to dismiss all of Hitler's followers as being simply stupid and immoral monsters is to make the same mistake of so many of their contemporaries, who badly underestimated them and lived to regret their mistake. If history teaches anything at all it is that intelligence is not identical with morality or for that matter even common sense. Furthermore, it should be remembered that Hitler succeeded not only in convincing intelligent Germans that he was a wise leader who would create a racial and economic utopia, he also convinced foreign leaders that he could be trusted. How else do we explain Nazi Germany's Concordat with the Vatican in 1933, the Polish-German Non-Aggression Pact of 1934, the Anglo-German Naval Pact in 1935, the Munich Agreement of 1938 or the Nazi-Soviet Non-Aggression Pact in 1939? To sign an international treaty requires trust that one's partner is honorable and will adhere to its terms.

Friedrich Rainer was one of those intelligent Nazis who trusted Hitler to create a utopian Aryan society. Rainer was never part of Hitler's inner circle. Nor did his name ever become a household word like Hermann Göring, Joseph Goebbels, Heinrich Himmler, or Rudolf Hess, to name just a few of the more notorious Nazis. Instead, Rainer's role as one of 40 *Gauleiters* made him a well connected "middle management" person.

Unlike so many other leading Nazis whose education was never completed, Rainer acquired an excellent knowledge of history in secondary school in the Klagenfurt, a hotbed of pan-German nationalism and the capital of Carinthia in southern Austria. Later he earned a law degree at the University of Graz in the equally nationalistic neighboring province of Styria. Born in 1903, he was too young to participate in the First World War, but he did join the military defense of Carinthia against Yugoslav incursions in 1918 and 1919. Already in 1927, Rainer read Hitler's *Mein Kampf* and three years later he helped found a local branch of the Austrian Nazi Party. He played no role in the Austrian Nazi *Putsch* of July 1934 that resulted in the murder of the Austrian Chancellor, Engelbert Dollfuss, but he did work to bring about a Nazi government in Austria in March 1938. Much to Rainer's chagrin, that government lasted all of one day before Germany annexed the country. However, he quickly reconciled himself to Austria's new status as the *Ostmark* of the Third Reich. As *Gauleiter* of Salzburg he worked to make the region the cultural center of the Third Reich. As the *Gauleiter* of an enlarged Carinthia between 1941 and 1945 he was in charge of Germanizing the Slovenes and defending the Reich from possible attacks from the south.

Friedrich Rainer thus played a significant role in the Third Reich. His post-war activities, however, were perhaps equally important. As one of the defense's witnesses at the Nuremberg trial of 1945 and 1946 for Arthur Seyss-Inquart—one of the architects of the Austro-German *Anschluss* of 1938 and later the Reich Commissar of occupied Holland—Rainer had a ringside seat at the proceedings. Not being on trial himself, and not knowing that he would later be tried and executed as a war criminal in Yugoslavia, he was able to take a relatively dispassionate view of the trial. His familiarity with the defendants, his knowledge of history, and his training as a lawyer as well as his ability to write clearly and succinctly, make his observations about the trial especially fascinating and valuable.

Rainer draws a vivid description of the cells of the prisoners and witnesses, their health care, exercise routine, hygiene, diet, reading material, and writing opportunities that are engrossing and justify Rainer's conclusion that treatment of the inmates was "good." Witnesses were carefully interrogated but never abused let alone tortured. Although they were kept in solitary confinement for months until after they had testified or been judged, every effort was made to prevent them from falling into "morbid" depression. Rainer's account leads to inevitable and unflattering comparisons with the American treatment of Iraqi and al-Qaeda prisoners at Guantanamo Bay in Cuba and the Abu Ghraib prison in Baghdad.

Rainer's overall assessment of the value of the trial is also interesting and thought provoking. He was not alone in pointing out the difficulty of German defense lawyers in obtaining pertinent documents or in criticizing the trial for using *ex post facto* laws instead of existing ones. Other critics have also agreed with Rainer that alleged war criminals ought to be tried only by judges from neutral countries that had not committed wartime acts for which the Germans were being tried. Although Rainer's criticisms have to be taken seriously, it is still worth remembering the Nuremberg trial was not a sham in contrast to Stalin's show trials of the 1930s. Three of the defendants were acquitted and only eleven of the twenty-one defendants received the death penalty. This outcome is a far cry from Stalin's proposal, momentarily seconded by President Roosevelt at the Teheran Conference in November 1943, that 50,000 German officers be shot at war's end. Moreover, the testimony and documents used in the trial, which filled

42 printed volumes, were enlightening to post-war Germans who were often ill informed about crimes committed by the Nazis. These volumes are also still of great value to historians today.

Maurice Williams has already provided new insights into the Nazi phenomenon with his exhaustively researched biography of Rainer: Gau, Volk, and Reich: Friedrich Rainer and the Paradox of Austrian National Socialism. His present work enlarges our knowledge of war crimes trials in general and the Nuremberg trial in particular. The document published for the first time here sheds much new and valuable information about the trial and is greatly enhanced by the inclusion of no fewer than 250 explanatory footnotes as well as valuable photographs, associated documents, and a map of the prison. All the people named by Rainer in his document are thoroughly identified by Professor Williams who also notes where Rainer's memory failed him. Readers will also be indebted to Williams for the detailed eight-page bibliography of materials related to the trial and its participants.

Bruce F. Pauley
Professor of History
University of Central Florida, Orlando

ACKNOWLEDGMENTS

The gracious help of able colleagues has made this publication possible and I am deeply indebted to them. To the linguistically gifted Römer family of Vienna, Austria (the late Dr. Wolfgang Römer, his wife, Dr. Beatrix Römer, and their daughter, Dr. Claudia Römer) I owe a major thank you. They provided the first working translation in English of Rainer's manuscript. As well they encouraged and inspired me to examine this era, despite their own misgivings and unpleasantries from the war and its aftermath. I am also thankful for the expertise of my colleague, Valerie Witham, as we examined this manuscript. Val was gracious with her time and skillful in her understanding of the linguistic nuances of Rainer and his phraseology. Her final translation superbly reflects Rainer's meaning and intent. Further, I wish to thank Adrian Ang who helped with the annotations and researched the background to the trial. Adrian undertook this work in one of my undergraduate directed studies courses and generously shared his findings; (Adrian is a promising young scholar who has just completed his Ph.D.). Magister Ljuba Dornik Šubelj of the Archives of the Republic of Slovenia first introduced me to the extensive collection of Rainer's papers. I am grateful for her help and her on-going support. Dr. Eric Nellis read several versions of the Introduction and offered valuable suggestions. I highly value both his criticisms and his encouragement, not just with this project but with my other work. Sylvie Zebroff provided invaluable assistance with the photographs and the formatting of this manuscript. As with other projects where Sylvie has helped me, it was a delight to work with her. I also wish to thank Okanagan University College (now the University of British Columbia Okanagan) for its generous financial support, both through the Professional Development Committee and the

Grants-in-Aid Committee, as well as the resources provided through a recent Sabbatical Leave. OUC was steadfast in supporting its faculty and their research. Finally, I save my biggest thank-you for my wife. Linda has helped me, supported me, encouraged me, run interference for me, and allowed me to spend the hours secreted away in the study. A simple "thank you" is never enough – but a special thank you is where I wish to begin.

CHRONOLOGY

Year	Rainer		Background to Nuremberg and the Internat'l Military Tribunal	
1903	23 Jul	Born, St. Veit an der Glan, Carinthia, Austria		
1938			13 Mar	Aust/German Anschluss
	May	Chief Nazi administrator for Salzburg		
1939			01 Sep	Germany invades Poland
1940			22 Jun	Fren surrender to Germans
1941			22 Jun	Germany invades USSR.
	Nov	Chief Nazi administrator for Carinthia and Carniola		
			11 Dec	Ger declares war on USA
1943	10 Sep	Adds responsibility for Adriatic Coastland		
1944			06 Jun	Normandy invasion
1945			Feb	Yalta, Allies decide to prosecute Axis leaders
			30 Apr	Hitler's suicide
			07 May	German unconditional surrender
	31 May	Captured by the British military		
			02 Aug	Nuremberg as trial site
			08 Aug	London Agreement
			12 Aug	War criminals arrive in Nuremberg
	24 Sep	Arrival Nuremberg as defense witness		
			19 Oct	Indictments issued
			20 Nov	Nuremberg war crimes trial begins

1946	12 Jun	First of two days testifying for Seyss-Inquart		
			30 Aug	Testimony ends
			01 Oct	Verdicts
			13 Oct	Appeals denied
			15 Oct	Göring's suicide
			16 Oct	Execution of 10 war criminals
			25 Oct	US estab Mil Tribunal for 11 subsequent Nuremberg trials
1947	13 Feb	Extradited to Yugoslavia		
			12 Mar	Truman Doctrine
	10 Jul	Trial begins in Ljubljana		
	18 Aug	Supposedly executed		
1948	Wrote Nuremberg account			
1950	Allegedly seen in 1952 in Serbia; executed (?)			

INTRODUCTION

Nearly six decades after the trial of the major Nazi war criminals, the Nuremberg process remains a landmark in international affairs.[1] It reflects the widely held view among anti-Nazis that National Socialism was not merely an evil system to overcome but also the instigator of heinous crimes which demanded punishment. By charging the most important surviving Nazis with crimes against peace, war crimes, crimes against humanity, and conspiracy, those heinous crimes could be examined and made public. By prosecuting and convicting the most important Nazis, punishment could then proceed. Thus, from November 1945 to October 1946 the surviving principals (and much of the world) listened as Allied prosecutors laid out evidence of grievous crimes, defense lawyers offered counter testimonials, and the several judges rendered their decisions. Eleven of the twenty-one tried were sentenced to death, three received life imprisonment, four were punished with varying prison terms while three were acquitted. The judgments also pronounced a number of organizations illegal and criminal: the Gestapo, the Defense Squads (SS), the Security Service (SD), and the Brown Shirts (SA). The Second World War, then, the most ruinous armed

[1] The full account of the trial was published in 42 volumes: International Military Tribunal, Trial of the Major War Criminals before the International Military Tribunal, Nuremberg, 14 November 1945 - 1 October 1946 (42 vols.; Nuremberg: International Military Tribunal, 1947). Two of the best accounts by Allied participants are Telford Taylor, The Anatomy of the Nuremberg Trial - A Personal Memoir (New York: Alfred A. Knopf, 1992) and Drexel Sprecher, Inside the Nuremberg Trial: A Prosecutor's Comprehensive Account. 2 vols. (New York: University Press of America, 1999). Accounts by German participants are much more critical, as in the memoirs and accounts of Karl Dönitz (London: Weidenfield and Nicolson, 1959), Franz von Papen (London: Andre Deutsch, 1952), and Hjalmar Schacht (Boston: Houghton Mifflin, 1956). Two valuable overviews are Ann and John Tusa, The Nuremberg Trial (New York: Atheneum, 1984) and Robert Conot, Justice at Nuremberg (New York: Harper and Row, 1983).

conflict in history, did not end as had earlier wars. Victory was followed by a legal assessment which rendered blame for the death and destruction.[2]

The International Military Tribunal (IMT) at Nuremberg also served other purposes. It introduced a major new concept to international affairs by transforming the individual from an *object* to a *subject* of international law. Individuals were now said to be liable for their actions without the benefit of immunity afforded by the doctrine that they were acting for the state.[3] This principle, emphasized by the IMT, has become an important tenet for the successors to Nuremberg: the 1993 tribunal dealing with war crimes in former Yugoslavia, the 1994 court for Rwanda, and most important, the International Criminal Court at The Hague.[4] These courts have confirmed that crimes on behalf of the state belong to individuals, thereby eliminating a mechanism whereby those individuals might escape their criminal actions.

Further, the IMT has served another purpose. For those who examine the National Socialist phenomenon, the process provides a wealth of public documentation on Hitler, his rise to power, and especially the planning,

---

[2] The legality of the major war criminals trial was based upon the London Charter, signed in August 1945 by the victorious Americans, British, French, and Soviets; the Charter also set the ground rules for the process. This first trial, of course, was not the only one which tried Nazis for war crimes; a series of later trials, also in Nuremberg, continued to assess blame and punish the lesser fry for crimes against peace and crimes against humanity. The 1945 process beginning in November was the largest and the most spectacular, however.

[3] The criminal responsibility of the defendants was determined in accordance with the maxim *actus non facit reum nisi mens sit rea* -- only an individual possesses a mind that may be filled with malicious intent at will. [See Albert G. D. Levy, "The Laws and Procedure of War Crimes Trials, " The American Political Science Review, XXXVII (December 1943): 1054.]

[4] In February 1993 the United Nations Security Council authorized the establishment of the International Tribunal for the Prosecution of Persons Responsible for Serious Violations of International Humanitarian Law Committed in the Territory of the Former Yugoslavia Since 1991. In November 1994 the Security Council adopted the Statute of the International Tribunal for Rwanda. The International Criminal Court (ICC), with a permanent seat at The Hague, Holland, was established in 2003. It prosecutes individuals accused of genocide, war crimes, and crimes against humanity.

launching, and execution of his war. To this day the Nuremberg Trial affords the most thorough record of those events.[5]

Along with these salutary considerations, however, the IMT has sparked considerable controversy. Critics have questioned its validity. The court lacked impartiality; it imposed *ex post facto* law; it prescribed victor's justice; it introduced a process only slightly better than summary executions. Other analysts have pointed to a severe imbalance between the prosecution and the defense, an imbalance which meant the accused had a decided disadvantage. Others have focused on the wisdom of individual verdicts. How does one reconcile death for one and imprisonment for another? Professional soldiers were especially uncomfortable with the military verdicts. Yet, the most telling criticism has focused on deterrence. Has the Nuremberg Trial deterred would-be aggressors?

The IMT has no shortage of defenders and critics. But regardless whether one supports or denounces the process, the importance of the trial itself is without question. It remains a landmark and controversial topic in international affairs. Thus, any previously unpublished materials demand to be added to the record and debate. What follows falls into that category.

In late 1947 or early 1948 Friedrich Rainer, a lawyer and Austrian Nazi, the *Gauleiter* and Governor of Carinthia from 1941 to 1945, and an ally of the leading figures in the Third Reich, wrote a treatise on the Nuremberg trial for his Yugoslav captors. Rainer, who had been captured by the British, had been summoned to the IMT as a witness for his *Anschluss* colleague, the defendant Arthur Seyss-Inquart, and had spent nearly eight months (October 1945 to June 1946) incarcerated in the witnesses' wing of the large complex where the process occurred.[6] There, he had observed the activities, personalities, and course of the

[5] The old standard, and still valuable, William Shirer, The Rise and Fall of the Third Reich: A History of Nazi Germany (New York: Simon and Schuster, 1960) makes extensive use of the Nuremberg trial documents. More recently Jackson Spielvogel in his text, Hitler and Nazi Germany: A History (4th ed.; Upper Saddle River, New Jersey: Prentice Hall, 2001) continues to encourage students to consult the proceedings and documents.

[6] After Nuremberg Rainer was interned by the Americans at Dachau before being turned

trial, firsthand observations about which the Yugoslavs were keen to have a record. In his account he gave his captors not only an idea on how that earlier trial had progressed but how it might be viewed in the future.

Rainer's Nuremberg discourse was part of a remarkable set of writings, all penned by this ex-*Gauleiter*, and all associated with his own trial. Convicted of crimes against the Slovene people in July 1947, Rainer was supposedly executed by the Yugoslavs shortly thereafter. He was, however, not punished as claimed. Instead he lived and worked for his captors for at least two years. From the summer of 1947 through late 1949, and probably into 1950, he wrote hundreds of pages of history, political commentary, regional studies, personality assessments, and personal recollections. One of the most important of these pieces focused on the Nuremberg Trial.[7]

Rainer's 80-page Nuremberg account provides a unique perspective on the process. As a witness who was not on trial himself, his testimony is more detached than the memoirs, for example, of the defendants Karl Dönitz, Hans Fritzsche, Franz von Papen, or Albert Speer. He provides a different perspective from that of the prosecutors David Maxwell-Fyfe and Telford Taylor. He had the advantage of direct participation which enables us to grasp some of the emotion that was involved. But his account also has the advantage of detachment since he was not himself charged with any crime at Nuremberg. Further, his rendition benefits because he was himself a lawyer.

Rainer's account is also unique because he attempted to write with the historian's eye, a perspective for which he had some experience. As a school boy, history had been his favorite subject. His teacher/mentor from 1914 to 1918 was

---

over to the Yugoslavs in February 1947 for trial.

[7] The bulk of Rainer's work, along with his trial records, are located in the Arhiv Republike Slovenije III (Archives of the Republic of Slovenia, Department III). It amounts to some 7000 pages of documentation. Other limited examples are available in London at The National Archives (Public Record Office) (TNA/PRO). See the author's Gau, Volk, and Reich: Friedrich Rainer and the Paradox of Austrian National Socialism (Klagenfurt, Austria: Verlag des Geschichtsvereines für Kärnten, 2005).

Martin Wutte, with whom Rainer maintained contact throughout his life. Wutte was a prominent Austrian historian. From him Rainer learned not just about the discipline of history but also about the importance of observing and noting detail. Throughout his life Rainer remained a keen observer, which he combined with a good memory for particulars. In his Nuremberg treatise those historical interests and habits took on special meaning. He wrote, of course, as a German nationalist, but he attempted to be objective and tried to distinguish between fact and rumor. He presented his evidence and then drew his conclusions. He endeavored to place his account in a larger context than the immediate trial. The result is an unusual piece of firsthand history as well as an important reminder that historical analysis belongs not just to the professional historian.

Rainer was not a particularly honorable or likeable person, but he was a skillful observer and an experienced political analyst. He was not a great writer, but his style is readable and informative. His treatise is not electrifying, but it provides new insight while complementing and extending our understanding of the Nuremberg process. At the same time we also acquire a glimpse into the mind, life, and story of Friedrich Rainer, a typical product of National Socialism, a man whose post-war writings, including his Nuremberg portrayal, clearly make him a Nazi apologist.

RAINER'S NUREMBERG ACCOUNT

This account of the International Military Tribunal was probably written in 1948 for Rainer's Yugoslav captors. Since officials of Tito's government had not been privy to the proceedings, a firsthand rendering from an eight month participant of the process was of considerable interest. Rainer's descriptions would help them understand better the mind, motivations, and methods of their recent enemy, as well as add to their knowledge of how the postwar powers viewed themselves and their world.

Rainer begins his account by providing details of the physical setting for the trial and the various personalities involved (both Allied and German). He then describes the atmosphere of the courtroom and the pressures, hopes and tensions experienced by the prisoners, and finally concludes with a lengthy analysis of the proceedings. He writes about the petty issues of prison which became so important to the once powerful of Germany (for example, what they could read and how often they could write letters). He describes the routine of prison life (the daily schedule, the food, the medical treatment, and the role of religion). He comments extensively on the United States involvement in the trial (Rainer did not like the way Americans interrogated prisoners but he said they provided good treatment and care). He tells of the background to the trial for the defendants - how they chose and worked with their legal counsel, how their evidence was extremely restricted, and how they were handicapped by the regulations of the London Charter.[8]

Aside from describing the setting and the personalities Rainer gives an excellent summation of the differences between the Anglo-Saxon criminal trial and the German or continental approach. He explains that the Nuremberg trial was conducted according to the principles of criminal trials current in England and the United States. He describes how that system worked and then how the continental system proceeded. What is most interesting is his conclusion. Others involved with the trial criticize the proceedings as unfamiliar and unfair, but Rainer, well acquainted and comfortable with the German-continental system (it was more likely to get to the "truth" under "normal circumstances"), argues that the American procedure was better, even preferred to the German system at Nuremberg; it permitted a real defense.

The most important part of this treatise, however, is the lengthy conclusion. Here Rainer considers the question: did the initiators of the trial

---

[8] The London Charter of August 1945 established the basis for prosecuting those accused of committing crimes during the war.

reach their aims? Yes, he argues, if the intent was to eliminate the top officials of the Third Reich; yes, if the intent was propaganda for the Allied victory. Doubtful, he asserts, if the intent was to clarify the question of war guilt; doubtful, if the intent was to avoid, impede, or humanize future wars; doubtful, if the intent was to enhance or strengthen international criminal law. Rainer expands upon each point. He also elaborates upon a larger issue, the morality of the entire process, particularly the role of the United States. Rainer found the moral approach of the Americans to the trial indefensible. He argued that they, as judges, could be accused of crimes similar to those laid against the Germans. He cites three examples to support this notion, examples which he asserts undermine the moral stance of the United States: the dropping of the atomic bomb on defenseless people in Japan, the treatment of the American Negro, and the failure of the United States to surrender to other governments anti-Communists who collaborated with the Nazis. Finally, Rainer argued against other war crimes trials because of strong and continuing sentiments of national sovereignty (most evident in the Cold War).[9]

That Rainer was not always correct in his several conclusions is obvious. Clearly, he was wrong on the issue of war guilt. He tried to argue that only German records had been examined, assuming that when allied accounts were studied, as after the First World War, the blame would be more equally shared. Rainer apparently was using his lesson of history, studying one conflict and applying its investigative results to another. Today, nonetheless, nearly 60 years later, after much study and extensive research, historians and other students of the

---

[9] In addition to his Nuremberg account Rainer also wrote on his imprisonment by the English (May to September, 1945) and on his internment by the Americans at Dachau (July 1946 to February 1947). These documents are not as arresting, however, as his Nuremberg account. See F. Rainer, "Meine Vernehmungen durch Engländer und Amerikaner" [My Interrogations by the English and the Americans], after 8.1947, n.pl. (Ljubljana, Slovenia?), and F. Rainer, "Das Internierungslager Dachau" [The Dachau internment camp], after 26.1.1948, n. pl. (Ljubljana?), both in Arhiv Republike Slovenije III (ARS-III), Ljubljana, Inv 761, 80-4, II-53 and II-54.

era continue to blame Nazi Germany for causing the war. What Rainer has really demonstrated is that there are no pre-determined certainties in historical studies.

On the other hand his doubts about how the trial results impeded, avoided, or humanized future wars has been correct. The precedent of the IMT punishing those responsible for war has not deterred others from engaging in military conflict. Since 1945 there have been at least 100 armed conflicts around the globe. Millions of people have died in the most horrific circumstances, and the value of destroyed property is incalculable. There are few "humane" aspects to these wars. The only thing about which Rainer erred was that recent warfare has not continued to be "total" and all the resources of the state have not been mobilized. For reasons not associated with any war crimes tribunal and possible punishments, wars have reverted to limited conflicts with limited objectives, mainly because the Cold War brought the possibility of nuclear annihilation. The principle of Mutually Assured Destruction meant that international wars would not be fought to the bitter end as in 1945.

Rainer's argument that international criminal law was not significantly strengthened by the IMT has some merit, but only in the short term. For a number of years there was no perceivable movement to bring charges against politicians and state leaders who conspired to make war, or actually waged war and perpetrated crimes against humanity. These wrongs as defined by the IMT continued unabated. Only in the 1990s did the Nuremberg precedent take on meaningful application. New tribunals appeared to judge war crimes in Yugoslavia and Rwanda, a head of state was held accountable for war time activities (Slobodan Milošović), and a permanent International Criminal Court was established. With these undertakings, international criminal law, using the IMT as a model, has clearly been enhanced and defined. On this issue, then, while Rainer erred in the long term, he reminds us that international law has not been easy to establish and its acceptance has not be immediate. He shows that frequently it takes time to acquire genuine legal precedence.

Further, in light of the more recent events in Iraq, including the capture of war criminals, especially Saddam Hussein, and the revelations of serious abuse by American and British soldiers on Iraqi prisoners, the question of morality raised by Rainer in 1947 retains its relevance. Can the actions of the victor in the aftermath of a war be considered just and morally right? After US authorities captured Saddam Hussein and contemplated how best to deal with his crimes against peace and crimes against humanity, how did they reconcile his deeds with their own actions in Iraq, especially their treatment of prisoners? Rainer was quite clear on that crucial issue in 1947: "The most general principle of any jurisdiction provides that a judge must himself be free of guilt. He himself must not have committed crimes of which he accuses somebody else." Rainer also implies another question in this statement and in his Nuremberg account: does the US, Great Britain, or any combination of states have the right to judge war crimes on behalf of victims who are not their own citizens?

Finally, Rainer correctly identified the major stumbling block to war crimes tribunals: national sovereignty. His point here has at least two considerations which states have emphasized, both stemming from fear. First, there was the fear that a higher authority would *impose* a law from the "outside." It took nearly 60 years to create a permanent International Criminal Court at The Hague because governments had to overcome their anxiety on this issue. Most nation states have now signed the treaty establishing the tribunal -- but not the government of the United States. It views the court as a threat to its national sovereignty. The absence of the US has not stood in the way of establishing the court or its deliberations, but American intransigence to participate constitutes a major disappointment and weakness.

As for the second consideration of the sovereignty issue, some states fear the *loss* of their right to do whatever is necessary to protect land and citizens. They continue to follow the old principle that "might makes right." This approach was clearly evident in the action of the American led invasion and occupation of Iraq, all in the name of a war on terror to defend the United States and according to President George W. Bush's doctrine of the pre-emptive strike. This same right to do anything necessary for defense also extended to other captives from Afghanistan incarcerated by the American government in Guantanamo Bay, Cuba. These detainees had little or no recourse to domestic US law, much less to the many provisions of international law which governed military captives. The government of the United States abandoned treaty obligations and international law, all in the name of self-interest and self-defense. National sovereignty, as Rainer rightly observed in 1947, deters the workings of international tribunals.[10]

At the end of his treatise Rainer ends on a more positive note as he outlines several principles which he feels would best serve future war crimes tribunals. He advocates: an international treaty to establish a court, a recognized body of international law defining war crimes which govern that court, neutral judges as presiding magistrates, and equal access for both prosecution and defense to the resources of the court. In 2003 these were some of the principles behind the International Criminal Court in The Hague. In the end, then, it is comforting to note that Rainer's legal training appears to take precedence over his belief in German national sovereignty. One may, however, prefer a much more cynical approach to this Nazi's account. As the vanquished, was Rainer not simply looking for a higher authority to take away the sting of losing, and override the power of the victor?

---

[10] On the domestic abuse of civil liberties in the US see Anthony Lewis, "Bush and the Lesser Evil," New York Review of Books 51.9 (27 May 2004). For further insight into the Guantanamo Bay incarcerations, see Gerald P. Fogarty, "Is Guantanamo Bay Undermining the Global War on Terror?" Parameters XXXV, #3 (Autumn 2005): 54-71.

RAINER'S CAREER

What sort of man was this Rainer? What were the influences on his life? How well placed was he in Hitler's hierarchy? How close was he to those about whom he writes? How reliable is he in this account?

Rainer was a highly ambitious and capable administrator, an able politician, a pan-German, and a Hitler loyalist to the end. He represented much that was characteristic of National Socialism. Born to a middle class family in Sankt Veit an der Glan, Carinthia, Austria, on 28 July 1903, he traced his lineage in this Germanic borderland back several centuries. His father, a middle school teacher, was an enthusiastic German, an official of the German-Democratic Party, and later an ardent supporter of the Greater German People's Party; the elder Rainer's strong sense of nationalism continued with his four children. Friedrich, the second of two sons, was the stereotype of the "German-Aryan": fair skin, blond hair, and blue eyes. He followed the usual educational route for the middle class, eventually graduating from university in Graz in 1926 with a doctorate in law. This schooling, added to his subsequent experience working in a legal firm, gave him crucial insight and an essential foundation to evaluate the procedural and legal matters at Nuremberg.[11]

He first showed nationalistic sentiments in 1919 and 1920 when he joined a local militia unit with his father and brother to protect Carinthia from the Slavic threat to the south. He worked hard to keep the Klagenfurt basin in Austria and

---

[11] Dr. jr. Friedrich Rainer, Jan.8, 1942, Archiv für publizistische Arbeit, Arbeiterkammer für Wien (AKW); "Die Ahnenheimat unseres Gauleiters Dr. Rainer," Wochenblatt der Landesbauernschaft Kärnten (Klagenfurt), July 22, 1944, Reichslandbund, Pressearchiv 256, Rainer, Bundesarchiv, Berlin-Lichterfeld (BA [B-L]); Lebenslauf, Personalnachweis Friedrich Rainer, formerly the Berlin Document Center, now incorporated in BA (B-L). (Hereafter cited as Lebenslauf, Rainer.) Vernehmungsniederschrift (Rainer interrogation before trial), 1947, ARS-III, Ljubljana, Slovenia, Inv 761, 80-4, II-8, 549; F. Rainer, "Über die Kärntner Slovenen-Frage," n.d. (after Jan. 26, 1948), ARS-III, Inv 761, II-8-b, 1376, 1378, 1389.

out of the new Yugoslavia.[12] He later joined other paramilitary groups and helped organize a military-like gymnastic group for the Carinthian province. In 1930 his enthusiasm for all things German was revealed when he joined the NSDAP.[13] This sense of German nationalism stayed with him throughout his life and served as an important backdrop to his Nuremberg account.

The abortive Nazi *putsch* of 1934 in which Chancellor Engelbert Dollfuss died and many party comrades were arrested and imprisoned gave the ambitious Rainer an opportunity to advance his standing in the hierarchy. The party, desperate for leaders, turned to young men like him and he became a key player in the illegal movement. He also became a confidant and close adviser to Arthur Seyss-Inquart, the Nazi sympathizer who later moved from cabinet minister to Austrian chancellor to governor of Holland and eventually to Nuremberg defendant. Rainer's testimony for Seyss-Inquart was the reason he spent eight months at the IMT, acquiring the firsthand knowledge for this account.

During the March 1938 crisis which led to *Anschluss*, Rainer played a crucial role in the actual takeover of his country by indigenous Nazis. He (and his close friend and collaborator, Odilo Globočnik) issued the orders to SS and SA units who then took control of government buildings. Further, while working with Seyss-Inquart, Rainer determined the composition of the new, albeit brief Nazi cabinet. His goal at the time was to create an independent, separate National Socialist state in Austria. He was surprised and clearly upset when Hitler announced the annexation of the country. As a loyal Nazi, nonetheless, Rainer put that disappointment behind him, especially since he soon acquired numerous honors and prestigious party posts.[14]

---

[12] Rainer, "Über die Kaerntner Slovenen-Frage," 1376; "Salzburg und sein Gauleiter Dr. Rainer," Voelkische Beobachter (Vienna), 3.7.1938, BA (B-L), Pers Rainer.

[13] K. Keinast, "Die Grossdeutsche Reichstag," June 1938, AKW; Lebenslauf, Rainer.

[14] Maurice Williams, "Delusions of Grandeur: The Austrian National Socialists," Canadian Journal of History XIV (Dec. 1979): 423, 427-428; Kienast, "Der Grossdeutsche Reichstag;" F. Rainer, "Report on the events in the NSDAP of Austria since the beginning of the last stage of battle until the seizure of power on the 11th March 1938," July 16, 1939, Document

By March 1938 he had also acquired an enviable reputation. A well-placed Reich official noted that he made an extraordinarily good impression. He was quiet, but had an inner passion. He displayed considerable intelligence and had a good understanding of his surroundings. He enjoyed considerable authority and had clearly done well advising Seyss-Inquart. Other colleagues considered him well bred and absolutely reliable, one who would always follow the party line. Another added that he spoke well in public. Everyone praised him for his diplomatic handling of people, so much so that he had earned the honorary acknowledgement as "foreign minister" of the Carinthian Nazis.[15] These same characteristics are seen in his Nuremberg account: intelligence, an understanding of his surroundings, a sense of authority, and a strong party orientation.

The clearest measure of his early success, however, came in May 1938 when Hitler appointed him head of the NSDAP in the Salzburg *Gau.* For the next three years Rainer established a reputation there as a strong administrator, a pronounced anti-cleric, and a champion of his region. He especially devoted considerable energy to his project of making Salzburg, already a city identified with music and the Baroque, into the cultural capital of the Third Reich.[16]

In the late summer of 1941 Hitler again recognized his accomplishments and rewarded him by sending him home to his native Carinthia. The youthful Nazi (he was 38) became *Gauleiter* and Governor there as well as Chief of the Civil Administration for Occupied Upper Carinthia and Carniola (the

---

PS812, in Nazi Conspiracy and Aggression, 10 vols. (Washington, D.C.: U. S. Government Printing Office, 1946-1948), 3:593-95; untitled memo (Odilo Globočnik?), May 1938, National Archives and Records Administration (NARA), College Park, Maryland, Microfilm No. T84, R16, frame 44270.

[15] Unterredung mit F. Rainer, March 1938, Handakten Megerle, Bd. NSDAP 5/5, 351687, Auswärtiges Amt, Bonn; Christian Opdenhoff an Bürckel, Vienna, April 2, 1938, Bundesarchiv, Koblenz, Schumacher 304; Peter Black, Ernst Kaltenbrunner: Ideological Soldier of the Third Reich (Princeton, N.J.: Princeton University Press, 1984), 80.

[16] Munzinger, Friedrich Rainer, 8 January 1942, Pressearchiv, AKW; Sigrid Löffler, "Aufstand der Provincz," *Profil,* 7 July 1938, AKW, File NSDAP-Salzburg; Ernst Hanisch, Nationalsozialistische Herrschaft in der Provinz Sazlburg im Dritten Reich (Salzburg: Landespressebüro, 1983), 77, 113, 129, 140-142.

northwestern part of today's Slovenia).[17] At his installation Hitler's deputy, Robert Ley, heralded him as the best appointment the *Führer* could have made.[18] Hitler also charged him with a specific task for the occupied territories: "Make this land German again."[19] Rainer devoted much of his attention to this goal, working closely with Heinrich Himmler to replace the local Slovene culture with one which was German.[20]

In 1943 when Mussolini's Italy collapsed and the Germans occupied the country, Hitler once more acknowledged Rainer and his talents. The *Führer* named him to head the new Operational Zone Adriatic Coastland, a territory composed of what is northeast Italy (including Trieste), the Istrian peninsula, and the Slovene region around Ljubljana. Nominally part of Mussolini's new puppet republic, Rainer made it a *de facto* German protectorate in which he held the power. The region was especially important as a bulwark protecting the underbelly of the Reich, a consideration which led him to build a major defense fortification from the sea to the Alps.[21]

By 1944, then, Rainer had become a prominent figure in Hitler's Germany, managing and leading an important segment of the Third Reich -- Carinthia, occupied Carniola, and the Adriatic Coastland. He had proven himself a capable

---

[17] Maurice Williams, "Friedrich Rainer, National Socialism, and Postwar Europe: The Historical World of an Austrian Nazi," Austrian History Yearbook XXX (1999): 111.

[18] Amtseinführung des Gauleiters (Rainer), durch den Reichsleiter Dr. Robert Ley am 29. und 30. Nov. 1942, NSDAP Hauptarchiv, Reel 6, Folder no. 143—Kärnten.

[19] Wilhelm Frick, in Trial of the Major War Criminals before the International Military Tribunal, 42 vols. (Nuremberg: International Military Tribunal, 1947-49), 20:363. (Main entry hereafter cited as Trial Major War Criminals.)

[20] Maurice Williams, "The Nazis, German Nationalism, and Ethnic Diversity: The Adriatic Coastland under Friedrich Rainer," Slovene Studies XVII, 1-2 (1995; published August 1998): 10-12.

[21] Cross-examination of Friedrich Rainer (in Slovene), July 1947, Fourth Yugoslav Army, Ljubljana, ARS-III, Fasc. 924, str. 62 (13), str. 66, str. 68 (16-17); Rainer an Bormann, Klagenfurt, December 18, 1944, BA (B-L), Globočnik.

administrator, self-assured, confident, and competent. He had further established himself as a loyal lieutenant to the *Führer* and the party. Even more than that he also revealed himself as a skillful politician, one who was especially well connected. His closest cohort was probably Heinrich Himmler, with whom he associated as local representative of the Reich Commission for the Strengthening of German Ethnicity (*Reichskommissar für die Festigung des deutschen Volkstums*, or RKFDV). He had close contacts with Hermann Göring because of the economic importance of his region. He saw Hitler frequently. His oldest comrade, Ernst Kaltenbrunner, had become head of the Security Service (*Sicherheitsdienst*, or SD) and successor to Reinhard Heydrich. Moreover, Rainer had always moved cautiously when dealing with others so that he had few meaningful enemies in the Third Reich. In short, his influence and importance reached into the highest levels of party and state.[22] These contacts, of course, later served him well at Nuremberg as he continued to talk to these people, or at least the survivors, and they introduced him to others who had served the Third Reich and its *Führer*.

By early spring 1945 as Germany's war descended into defeat, Rainer's administrative and political successes, like those around him, began to crumble. He consequently abandoned most of his responsibilities, except for his native Carinthia. Here he did everything possible to preserve the unity of his home province and prevent its division or annexation by the advancing Slovene partisans. In this he succeeded, aided by tough German resistance to the southern invaders, light opposition toward the British (enabling them to enter Klagenfurt first), his own timely resignation, and considerable luck. But he succeeded. Although he was captured by the British, he accomplished his final objective of

[22] F. Rainer, "Organizacija komisarja za drzavno obrambo," ARS-III, Inv. 761, 80-4, II-35, 1780-84; Josef Vogt, "Karakteristika in delovanje Gauleiterja Rainerja," ARS-III, Inv. 761, 80-4, II-2, 398-405; Interrogation of Josef Vogt before July 1947 trail (in German), Ljubljana (?), May 1947 (?), ARS-III, Inv. 761, 80-4, III-6, 3579.

maintaining a unified Carinthia. Greater Germany may have disintegrated, but not his Carinthia.[23]

Rainer spent the rest of his life in prison, first with the British, then with the Americans, and at the end with the Yugoslavs. The British detained him for nearly five months, conducting extensive interviews and receiving detailed reports on his activities. In October he went to Nuremberg where he served as a witness in defense of his old colleague Seyss-Inquart. His testimony focused on the events leading to *Anschluss*. While there he also wrote an extensive essay, addressed to his old mentor Martin Wutte, justifying his activities as Carinthian *Gauleiter* and Governor. Further, he carefully noted the detail of the trial and expanded his knowledge of the Third Reich through conversations with colleagues, old and new, who passed through his Nuremberg prison. This knowledge is clearly evident in the following account. From July 1946 until February 1947, the Americans interned him at Dachau where he had a chance to flee with a fellow *Gauleiter*, but he refused since he saw that his escape would be seen as an admission of guilt. He expected to be tried, of course, but thought that any process would occur in Carinthia. He was surprised in February 1947 when two Yugoslav officers arrived to escort him to Slovenia. The Americans had agreed to release him to the Yugoslavs. His subsequent trial in Ljubljana, before a military court, took place in July and focused on his crimes: murder, property destruction, and acts of terror against the Slovene people. He tried to downplay his role and even shift blame to others. He claimed friendship with the Slovenes, but to no avail. He and eleven co-defendants received death sentences.[24]

---

[23] Maurice Williams, "Friedrich Rainer e Odilo Globocnik. L'amicizia insolita ed I ruoli sinistri di due nazisti tipici," Qualestoria (Trieste) XXV (1997): 169-175; Report on conversations between F. Rainer and S. Uiberreither, CSDIC Austria, September 16, 1945, 1 SC/CSDIC/X 9, TNA/PRO, WO 204/11505.

[24] F. Rainer, "Meine Vernehmungen durch Engländer und Amerikaner;" Karl Höffkes, Hitlers politische Generale: Die Gauleiter des Dritten Reichs (Tübingen: Grabert Verlag, 1987), 262; Rainer testimony, Trial Major War Criminals, 16:123-149; material from Rainer's 1947 trial in Ljubljana, ARS-III, Inv. 761, 80-4. See also Alfred Elste, Michael Koschat, and Hansi Filipič, NS-Österreich auf der Anklagebank: Anatomie eines politischen Schauprozesses im

The end of Rainer's life is a mystery. According to his death certificate and several official accounts, the sentence was carried out in August 1947. There were stories at the time, however, that he did not die then. Apparently, the Yugoslavs had a special prison where they kept ranking Nazis, including those who had been convicted and sentenced to death. In Rainer's case he possibly stayed in this prison working with the local authorities, writing hundreds of pages of history, analysis, and opinion. His surviving documentation makes it quite clear he did not die until at least early 1950.[25]

RAINER'S PERSONALITY

Further analysis of Rainer's personality will help put his Nuremberg treatise into a clearer perspective. He was obviously an egotist; he had delusions concerning his character, arguing that he was an honorable Nazi; and despite the assertion of absolute loyalty to Hitler, he became a collaborator.

First, the man had an exceptionally strong opinion of himself. That becomes obvious from his manner, his methods, and his musings, especially in this account of Nuremberg. Yet, in many respects he had a right to that ego. As noted, at the youthful age of 34 he was *Gauleiter* of Salzburg, a post which made him one of Hitler's important lieutenants and placed him clearly in the presence of his *Führer*. (Salzburg was in the valley immediately beneath Hitler's mountain retreat of Obersalzburg.) At 38 he moved on to become master of the southern fiefdom of Carinthia and the adjacent lands of Upper Carniola. Two years later,

---

kommunistischen Slowenien (Klagenfurt: Hermagoras Verlag, 2000).

[25] Federativna Ljudska Republika Jugoslavija, Izpisek iz mrlišne knijige, April 1, 1952, and Dr. A. Wiehs an Dr. Leopold Jungfer, Vienna, October 2, 1975, both reproduced in Lo sterminio mancato: La dominazione nazista nel Veneto orientale 1943-1945, ed. Pier Arrigo Carnier (Milano: Mursia, 1982); Elio Apih, "Tre documenti sulla politica nazista nel litorale adriatico," Movimento di Liberazione in Italia XXXIV (1972); Höffkes, Hitlers politische Generale, 262-263; Nikolaus von Preradovic, Österreichs Höhere SS-Führer (Berg am See: Kurt Vowinchel-Verlag, 1987), 73; interview with Mag. Ljuba Dornik Šubelj, Archivist, ARS-III, October 1996.

after the demise of Mussolini, Hitler selected him to head the operation zone centered in Trieste, a region which protected the southern underbelly of the Reich. In addition, he met frequently and corresponded often with the major political figures of Greater Germany, consulted regularly with key military figures, and represented the Reich in neighboring territories. Although he was not part of the inner circle, he was clearly one of Hitler's chief subordinates. In May 1945 he was only 41 years of age.

The British who captured him acknowledged his egotism. "Dr Rainer is a man of some intelligence and energy who played a considerable part in the events leading up to the Anschluss. He is vain and self-opinionated, however."[26] A further anecdote reinforces that view. The same English captors frequently taped secretly his conversations with his roommate. During one August 1945 recording, Rainer was discussing the new Austrian political situation. He had been asked to write an essay on the future of the country and he thought he saw a role in it for himself. In his musings, he exclaimed, "Come to think of it: the RENNER Cabinet - the RAINER Cabinet - only a small change required!"[27]

Rainer also had a peculiar sense of his own moral character, a delusion which did not necessarily correspond to reality. He argued that he was a "decent" Nazi[28] and sincerely felt his captors would consider his abilities and would call upon him to play a role in the new Austria. He could not imagine himself labeled a war criminal, a message which is abundantly clear in this Nuremberg account.

---

[26] "Austria; A Gauleiter's Views on the Future," Austria, Joint Weekly Intelligence Summary, Nov. 16, week ending 27 Oct 45, TNA/PRO, FO 1007/300.

[27] Conversation between F. Rainer and S. Uiberreither, No. 1, Sub-Centre, Combined Services Detailed Interrogation Centre (CSDIC) Austria, 20 Aug 45, 1 SC/CSDIC/X 5, p. 7, TNA/PRO, WO 204/11505.

Karl Renner was the head of the provisional government in Austria after the collapse of the Third Reich; he later became the first president of the Second Austrian Republic.

[28] F. Rainer, "Meine Vernehmungen durch Engländer und Amerikaner," n.d. (after July 1947), n.pl. (Ljubljana?), ARS-III, Inv 761, II-53," 2847.

Rainer also argued that there were many other decent Nazis in Austria.

On numerous occasions he voiced these sentiments. One month after his capture, Rainer proclaimed: "There's one thing we can rely on quite confidently: that we, with our ability and our good reputation, will, within a reasonable space of time, be asked to take over certain jobs."[29] In early August he exclaimed, "One day they'll summon me, perhaps the British Conservatives, or somebody else, maybe in five years, or in eight, or perhaps even ten years, but they'll do it."[30] By early September, he was saying, "I think it quite probable that they'll release me, and perhaps even allow me to work again as a notary. . . . I don't even consider political rehabilitation impossible."[31] Then he asserted, "I would never have dreamt that I would be accused of being a war criminal."[32] But the key statement regarding his claim to decency came on 11 October 1945 after finding out he was to go to Nuremburg. Thinking that he would be on trial, he said, "How absurd that we should face our trials just when there's general reconstruction and cooperation in AUSTRIA. In itself it might not actually be a bad thing. It would be bad if only people like [Hans] FRANK were tried. Decent Nazis ought to appear in court too."[33] And he added, "In my own case my idealism and my clean ways of living might be used to great advantage by the defence."[34] But it was not his "decency," "idealism," or "clean ways of living" which made his time at Nuremberg meaningful; it was his observations, his grasp of detail, and his

---

[29] Conversations of Friedrich Rainer, Siegfried Uiberreither, Siegfried Kasche, Tobias Portschy, Alois Maier-Kaibitscsh, and Otto Modrinak, 1 July 1945, CSDIC/CMF/X 188, p. 1, TNA/PRO, WO 204/11505.

[30] Conversations between F. Rainer and S. Uiberreither, No. 1 Sub-Centre, CSDIC, Austria, 15 August 1945, 1 SC/CSDIC/X 4, p. 4, TNA/PRO, WO 204/11505.

[31] Report of conversation between Rainer and Uiberreither, No 1, Sub-Centre, CSDIC Austria, 16 September, 1 SC/CSDIC/X 9, p. 3, TNA/PRO, WO 204/11505.

[32] Report on conversations between Rainer & Uiberreither, OC No 1 Sub Centre, CSDIC, BTA, CMF, 3 October 1945, 1 SC/CSDIC/X 11, p. 2, TNA/PRO, WO 204/11505.

[33] Report on conversation between Rainer & Ulberreither, No 1 Sub Centre, CSDIC, 16 October 1945, 1 SC/CSDIC/X 13, pp. 2-3, TNA/PRO, WO 204/11505.

[34] Ibid., 6.

analytical abilities, all combined with the opportunity to write this account for the Yugoslavs. These things, not decency, set him apart and make his Nuremberg story meaningful.

There was also another side to his personality. Despite an assertion of total loyalty to Hitler he quickly became a collaborator when the war ended. Seemingly, he had taken his direction from the *Führer*, had given absolute obedience to his leader, and had obeyed his successor to the very end. Rainer's faith was such that as late as mid-April 1945, he was telling his associates that there was still hope of victory.[35] Even after his capture he continued to express great faith in Hitler as one of the pre-eminent figures of history.[36]

Yet within hours of his confinement Rainer was working with the British, providing both oral and written information. At one point his captors asked him to comment on various personalities who were then working with the new provincial government of Carinthia. Rainer agreed to make the assessments even though he knew his comments would damage or destroy any future in government for these men. He wrote numerous pieces for the British military -- accounts of defense fortifications, comments on personalities, assessments of the political situation, and predictions for the future.[37] The British soon called him "an opportunist of the first water."[38] And he continued his cooperation with the Americans and the Yugoslavs, writing hundreds of pages with his views on the history, organization,

---

[35] Gauleiter Rainer bei einer Tagung politischer Leiter am 18.April 1945 in Krainburg, in August Walzl, Kärnten 1945 (Klagenfurt: Universitätsverlag Carinthia, 1985), 78.

[36] Conversations between Friedrich Rainer, Siegfried Uiberreither, and Tobias Portschy, No. 1, Sub-Centre, CSDIC Austria, 2 August 1945, 1 SC/CSDIC/X 1, pp. 2-3, TNA/PRO, WO 205/111505; CSDIC/ X 9, p. 5.

[37] F. Rainer, "Meine Vernehmungen durch Engländer und Amerikaner," 2836-37, 2841, 2845, 2851.

[38] E. Passant, Research Department, Foreign Office, 20 November 1945, TNA/PRO, FO 371/46682.

and activities of the Third Reich, plus his analysis of numerous people both in old Germany and new Austria. The Nuremberg account is one of those pieces.[39]

Collaboration then, or cooperation if we wish to soften it, appeared as Rainer's major trait after May 1945. But was it simply "collaboration," or was there another explanation for his action? One mitigating consideration was to note that although Rainer had been a Hitler loyalist, he was not a diehard fanatic prepared to fight on when all hope had vanished. He had no intention of killing himself for the Nazi cause. Among other things, he said he had a family of eight children to consider, one of whom was born after his capture. That family, and all families, he proclaimed on several occasions, were important and should be nurtured.[40] In his last conversation with his friend Odilo Globočnik, for example, the two men agreed that a chief value of National Socialism that had to be preserved was the "simple and natural family life."[41] He, a father, had a duty to survive for his family.

Another plausible explanation for his action was the view of himself as a "decent" Nazi who had nothing to hide. To Rainer National Socialism was an experiment which had failed, or perhaps, a state whose time had not yet come, or possibly, a realm which would someday re-emerge.[42] As he saw it, it was a first attempt at a state organized on the basis of "laws for living" (*lebensgesetzlicher Grundlage)*,[43] not an evil ideology which had caused extensive death, destruction,

[39] The Yugoslavs apparently knew of Rainer's analytical and writing abilities as well as his cooperative manner since the British, and probably the Americans, routinely turned over complete files when they released prisoners to other governments.

[40] CSDIC/X 1, pp. 4-5; CSDIC/X 9, p. 3; CSDIC/X 13, pp. 2 & 5, 8; CSDIC/X 7, p. 1; Gesichtspunkte für ein Gnadengesuch (Dr. Rainer), ARS-III, Inv. 761, 804, II-5, 419; Conversation between Friedrich Rainer and Siegfried Uiberreither, 28 July 1945, CSDIC/CMF/ X 197, p. 9, TNA/PRO, WO 204/11505; CSDIC/X 11, p. 5.

[41] CSDIC/ X 3, p. 4.

[42] F. Rainer, "Meine Vernehmungen durch Engländer und Amerikaner," 2835-36; CSDIC/X 5, p. 3; CSDIC/X 3, p. 3; CSDIC/X 4, p. 4; CSDIC/X 9, p. 3.

[43] F. Rainer , "Über nationalsozialistische Propaganda," n. d. (after June 1948), n.pl. (Ljubljana?), ARS-III, Inv. 761, 80-4, II-40, 2160. See also CSDIC/X 1, p. 4; CSDIC/X 7, p. 5.

and tragedy. As one of the good, decent Nazis, and as a man with a sense of history, he had a responsibility to tell the story of National Socialism so future generations could properly judge its place in history. Consequently, Rainer felt he had nothing to hide, and need show neither regret nor remorse for his actions.[44] His essay on Nuremberg is a testament to this notion.

Of course, after his July 1947 trial, he had another motivation to explain his collaboration: the desire to live, or at least, a desire to die decently. Rainer's sentence stipulated death by hanging. As long as he continued to write for the Yugoslavs, he was useful and death could be deferred. Postponement might even bring a change of circumstances which could modify his condition. Or if he was going to die, at least Rainer hoped the method would change from the rope to a firing squad.[45] Rainer therefore became the worker, the writer who collaborated with his captors and authored hundreds of pages of history, analysis, recollections, and observations. Among those pieces is his unique eyewitness report on the Nuremberg trial.

---

[44] Rainer , "Über nationalsozialistische Propaganda," 2160; CSDIC/X 197, p. 8; CSDIC/X 5, p. 5; CSDIC/CMF/X 188, p. 1; CSDIC/X1, p. 5; CSDIC/X 3, p. 2; CSDIC/X 11, p. 6; CSDIC/X 13, p. 6.

[45] CSDIC/X 4, p. 3; CSDIC/X 7, p. 2; CSDIC/X 9, p. 3; CSDIC/X 13, p. 7; Gesichtspunkte für ein Gnadengesuch (Dr. Rainer), 419.

Editor's note:

Rainer's long paragraphs have been divided into shorter ones to make easier reading. Further, his postscript, containing details he remembered after writing the manuscript, has been moved to a more logical place just before the final analysis.

The Nuremberg War Crimes Trial and Its Side Effects[1]

Contents	Page

[1] Rainer's title for his manuscript. His Table of Contents follows with the original page numbers. The numbers in brackets [ ] refer to the page numbers in this edition.

[page 1]

Dr. Friedrich Rainer

The Nuremberg War Crimes Trial and Its Side Effects

After the collapse and after a short stay at a camp, I was interned by the English at the Jerolitsch Inn near Klagenfurt together with *Gauleiter* Dr. Uiberreither.[2] The more important persons from Carinthia and Styria were sometimes brought there from the camps and interrogated. The two of us were always there. On 1 October 1945, the section moved together, including ourselves, to the Lassnitzhoehe sanatorium near Graz, probably because this building could be heated. On 11 October 1945, the manager of the office informed us that the International Commission for the Verification of War Crimes[3] had ordered our transfer to Nuremberg. On 12 October 1945, we were taken to Salzburg by car and handed over to the Americans at the provincial prison. They locked us up in a cell. On 24 October 1945, around noon, an American officer from Nuremberg in a Marine uniform came and took us in a private car to Nuremberg. We arrived there after 7 p.m. when it was already dark.

After passing a guard at the entrance, we came into a courtyard and then stopped in front of the narrow side of a building that looked like a church. It was the southwestern wing of the so-called cell block. The cell block was the Nuremberg interrogation centre and belonged to a big complex of law courts in the northwestern part of the city.[4] Part of it had been destroyed by bombs. The

---

[2] Sigfried Uiberreither (1908- ?) served as *Gauleiter* (1938-1945) and *Reichsstatthalter* (1940-1945) of neighboring Styria, and Chief of the Civil Administration for Lower Styria (1941-1945). He escaped Allied custody in May 1947, fleeing to South America.

[3] Rainer's name for the United Nations War Crimes Commission.

[4] The defendants and witnesses held in protective custody were housed in the Nuremburg City Jail, attached to the Palace of Justice. Defendants and witnesses entered the court via a covered runway so that they did not leave the secure area. The same troops guarded both the defendants and the witnesses.

main building and the cell block, too, had been hit, but most parts of the houses were still useable. In the main building there were interrogation rooms and **[page 2]**[5] the court room. The cell block was separated by a high wall and stood isolated in a huge area. Its bigger part was cultivated as a garden plot, and the Americans had built a wooden wall to separate it from the two exercise yards reserved for the prisoners' use. There was a passage way between the cells and the main building which could be reached through an iron door in the wall. The surrounding wall was equipped with sentry posts and a connecting corridor. American guards stood there with sub-machine guns.

The cell block consisted of four wings, each of which contained about 100 individual cells. The wings were positioned at a 60 degree angle to each other around a central observation post from which there was a clear view of the whole length of each wing. The Americans had isolated each wing with a continuous wooden wall and had closed down the observation post. The two outer wings formed a straight line running from the northeast to the southwest. The main frontage, which was opposite the back of the main building, faced northwest. The church was built between the two wings at a right angle facing northwest. In the southwestern wing, the main defendants and some of the witnesses were housed. In the neighboring wing to the east were the majority of the witnesses, and for this reason it was named the witnesses' wing. The living quarters for the guards and the staff were in the third and fourth wings. The rectangle between the southwestern wall of the church, the northwestern wall of the defendants' wing, the wooden corridor, and **[page 3]** the wall served as an exercise yard for the inmates of the defendants' wing. The sector between the defendants' wing and the witnesses' wing, which was separated from the garden area by a wooden fence, served as an exercise yard for the occupants of the witnesses' wing. Both exercise yards were grassed and had paving stone walkways and beautiful old trees. In the

---

[5] These page number notations indicate the beginning of the page in Rainer's original manuscript.

exercise yard for the occupants of the witnesses' wing there was a gymnasium built from light weight materials, in which, from time to time, the American guards and we also played basketball. On 16 October 1946, those sentenced to death were hanged there.

We entered the defendants' wing through the door at the southwestern narrow side and found ourselves in a high narrow room that looked like the nave of a church. It was brightly lit by electric lights. On both sides there were three stories of narrow iron walkways, which reminded me of the inside of the huge engine room on the steamship *Rex*.[6] On these there were American guards with helmets on their heads (made of pressed paper or cork) and leather clubs in their hands. Along the wall one could see cell doors. Each door had a piece of paper with a name written on it, and beneath it, the wooden cover for the opening through which food was passed, was hanging down and one could see that inside it was pitch-black. While passing through the ground floor, I was quickly able to read the names of some of the main defendants. Dr. Frank[7] had propped up a book against the wooden cover which he had pushed open, and used the lighting from the hallway to read. Dr. Frick[8] stuck his head through the opening to see who was coming. The others could not be seen in the darkness of their cells.

We were led into an office on the right hand side of the ground floor. **[page 4]** We had to put down our luggage and undress completely. A sergeant searched our clothes. Meanwhile a slender white-haired man came in, greeted us amiably and shook hands with each of us. He was the German prison doctor, Dr. Pflücker,[9] normally a doctor at the spa of Bad Wildungen.[10] He asked about our

---

[6] A German naval vessel, docked in Triest, which Rainer had visited as head of the Operational Zone Adriatic Coastland.

[7] Hans Frank (1900-1946), the Nazi party's leading jurist, was Governor-General of that part of German occupied Poland not incorporated into the Reich.

[8] Wilhelm Frick (1877-1946) was the Minister of the Interior from 1933 to 1943. After that he served as Reich Protector of Bohemia and Moravia.

[9] Dr. Ludwig Pflücker, an elderly neurologist from Nuremberg, was a German Prisoner of

health, took our pulse, and promised to visit again tomorrow. Then we were separated. Uiberreither was taken to the second floor, and I was given a dark solitary cell on the third floor in the same wing. I groped around and found that the toilet was in the right corner and the iron bed with a mattress and several good American blankets was against the left wall. The narrow cell window was blocked with a mesh of wire and glass. It was closed. The cell was well heated.

After 7 o'clock the next morning, a German attendant passed me my breakfast, an American bowl full of sweet porridge. Later on, another German brought a broom, a dustpan, and water to wash. Meanwhile, it had become light enough for me to inspect the cell. It measured about three by five meters and was fairly high. The floor was paved with simulated stone slabs. The moveable furnishings consisted of a small table made of thin narrow pieces of wood with a cardboard top just about strong enough to hold the food or a few books. That's all there was. Everything else, cupboards, the mirror, the wooden table, the chair, the clothes peg, the lamp and the cable had been removed, even the wooden boards for sitting that had been screwed to the toilet bowl had been taken away. Previous inmates had put some matches into the resulting nail holes, and they served as dubious means for hanging up a towel or jacket. **[page 5]** Everything else had to be put on the floor. A steam pipe running the length of one wall provided heat. A stick, passed to you from the outside, was used to open the window. It was impossible to look out. Shortly after breakfast Mr. Otto Streng,[11] the librarian, came and brought a novel about the Matterhorn as his first offering and wrote down my reading requests. Dr. Pflücker came and examined me. Then an

---

War employed as physician to the defendants. He spoke English and lived in the prison where he was available 24 hours a day.

[10] Bad Wildungen, a spa city more than 700 years old, is about 200 kilometers northwest of Nuremberg.

[11] Otto Streng, a 45-year-old Berliner, was another German POW employed as prison librarian, mailman, and interpreter. He, like Pflücker, was on call 24 hours a day, and like other POW's working in the prison, was chosen for his professional skill and his non-party background.

American brought some of my personal things, underwear, books, papers, and toiletries. A German interpreter announced the visit of the prison commander, Colonel Andrus,[12] and told me to stand up straight. Then Andrus, who immediately visited each new inmate, came. He is of medium height, stocky, and a well nourished man between 50 and 60, with a heavy walk and a strict manner like a *Gymnasium*[13] professor. I think he also wears glasses. He was wearing the American uniform with long trousers and low shoes, which would have looked like brown civies, were it not for some badges on the collar, the chest and sleeves, which gave them a military look. He also wore the paper helmet, highly polished, which looked rather comical in light of his quite unmilitary appearance. He only spoke English and used the interpreter. He asked for my name and birthplace and whether I was a National Socialist. When I answered yes, he said he was sorry. Since I could not think of a suitable answer, I was quiet. Then he asked whether I wanted a Bible. I said no. He shook his head again as if I were a lost cause and went away. Thus the ceremonies of admission were finished.[14] I will now give my account of the proceedings.

The most outstanding facility was the library. It was the old prison library from which only the Nazi-literature **[page 6]** had been removed. It contained nearly all the good literature in German, works of foreigners in German translation, several annual volumes of humorous and art journals, as well as books in English and French. Every day the librarian Streng, a prisoner of war from Berlin, made a tour of the cells and exchanged books. One could also read

---

[12] Colonel Burton C. Andrus, known as a "spit-and-polish stickler," had had experience with the army stockade in Fort Oglethorpe, Georgia. After Nuremberg he retired from the army and became a geography and business administration professor at the University of Puget Sound, Tacoma, Washington; he died in 1977 at the age of 85.

[13] A secondary school of the highest order designed to prepare students for university.

[14] By December 1945 the routine for arriving witnesses confined to Nuremberg was standardized. They received three orientation memos: Rules for Prisoners, Prison Routine, and Regulations on letter and postcard writing. In addition a new personnel file, the 201 file, was set up. See the Appendix for examples of the orientation memos.

several books at one time for variety. Newspapers were not to be had in solitary confinement, but they were allowed in the witnesses' wing. The Catholic clergyman Father Sixtus[15] looked after them.

In the beginning, food was excellent. Breakfast consisted of porridge, several kinds of cream of wheat and groats,[16] all of them sweetened with plums or raisins. For lunch there was a mug of hearty beef soup, then a bowl full of meat, potatoes, vegetables and gravy, and afterwards often a bowl of apricot or plum compote or a dessert with a sauce. At lunch and dinner you were allowed to take as many slices of bread as you wished. At 2 p.m. there was a mug of real coffee or tea. At suppertime there was porridge, or some vegetables, or a cake dessert, or bread and jam, or cheese, along with coffee or tea. The cook and some of the kitchen staff were prisoners of war from Vienna, so that the cuisine was familiar to us Austrians. In the spring of 1946 the quality and quantity of food started to diminish significantly.[17] Desserts were abolished. There was only substitute coffee and a little bread. Inmates lost weight. My loss amounted to 8 kilos. It was the fault of the administration that we lived from hand to mouth and were left without anything after the American provisions had been consumed.

The medical command was in the hands of two American doctors,[18] **[page 7]** both of them Jews, but efficient, considerate and friendly. They performed operations and in special cases they came to the cells. Dr. Pflücker carried out the daily medical care with discretion and efficiency. Every day he

[15] Father Sixtus O'Connor was assigned by the US army to minister to the spiritual needs of the six Roman Catholic defendants. Young, energetic, a great sports fan, and very popular with the internees, he occasionally broke the rules and helped prisoners contact their families.

[16] Hulled, crushed grain, usually made from oats.

[17] From December 1945 through mid-February 1946, for example, the prisoners ate a great deal of hash and had few desserts. See Appendix for sample daily menus.

[18] Lieutenant Charles Roska from Ohio and Lieutenant Roy Martin from Kentucky cared for the prisoners until the end of the trials and were then present at the executions. Martin published the account of his work at Nuremberg as Inside Nürnberg: Military Justice for Nazi War Criminals (Shippensburg, Pennsylvania: White Mane Books, 2000).

visited each of the prisoners in solitary confinement. He also saw the defendants several times a day. He adhered strictly to his instructions. As proof of his trustworthiness he received a key to the cells so he could enter without a guard. He was the only German with whom prisoners were permitted to speak during solitary confinement. I remember with gratefulness this kind-hearted, untiring old gentleman. There was also a German dentist[19] there, who was assisted by some of the orderlies. On the third floor they had taken out the wall between two cells and turned this double cell into a kind of walk-in clinic for x-rays, heat treatments and massage. On Fridays each prisoner was weighed. The people who brought food were instructed to report the prisoners who were not eating. Once when I did not eat because of an upset stomach, the American doctor came within half an hour and asked what was the matter. They took extensive precautions to prevent further suicides. After *Reichsgesundheitsführer* (Reich Leader for Health) Dr. Conti[20] had hanged himself from the window, the cells were cleared as I have described already. After that no shoelaces or drawstrings in clothes were allowed. Cardboard tables had been made so that it was not possible to climb on them anymore.

The corridors and the spiral staircases were covered with wire mesh so that one could not jump down. Each sentry was responsible for five cells and had to walk back and forth continuously and look into the cells through the food opening. During the night the sentries had powerful flashlights **[page 8]** which they directed into the cells each time they passed which was nearly every 30 seconds. This was intensely disturbing. Once you woke up, you needed some trick to fall asleep again. That is why there was a great increase in the use of sleeping pills. The sentries changed every two hours. They were soldiers from regular regiments in Germany. Every month replacement units were sent,

---

[19] Dr. Heinz Hoch from Bonn, another German POW, had been with the chief prisoners since their first internment at Mondorf-les Bain, Luxembourg.

[20] Leonardo Conti (1900-1945) had had the original responsibility for the euthanasia program. On 6 October 1945 he hanged himself in his cell, the first of the three suicides at

although one unit was permanently stationed there.[21] At the beginning there were still some soldiers who had taken part in the war, but then more and more, recruits would come. On the whole they were rather good natured fellows, badly trained and bad mannered. They were lazy and careless in their duties which helped temper much of the prescribed harshness. Colonel Andrus used to observe them intensely and punish them because of minor infractions in their guard duties.[22] On Sundays and Mondays they were especially in need of sleep so in the witnesses' wing, where the atmosphere was more relaxed, they had become accustomed to our watching for the Colonel or the person in charge while the guard slept it off in the cell. In the defendants' wing, however, the scene was not so pleasant. There was even stricter enforcement when, about a week after our arrival, despite all the precautions, Dr. Ley[23] succeeded in strangling himself by making a rope out of a piece of underwear, attaching it while sitting on the toilet, and throwing himself forward. After this trick the main defendants, who were housed on the ground floor, were each assigned a guard who had to look continuously into the cell, even during their private moments. Göring[24] used to converse pleasantly with his guard while he sat on the throne.

Nuremberg; the others were Robert Ley and Herman Göring.

[21] The permanent unit responsible for security at Nuremberg was Andrus' command, the 6850th Internal Security Detachment. Although the unit was permanent Andrus, complained that his turnover exceeded 600 percent for enlisted men and 125 percent for officers, numbers which meant he never had enough well trained guards nor experienced officers to lead the detachment.

[22] The extensive directions for the guards included the pronouncement that "failure to obey will be considered a court-martial offence." William Glenny, one of the guards, observed, after hearing the regulations, "All these rules. I'm looking at the colonel and I'm saying [to myself], 'This man's out of his mind.' But, you have to take orders." [William Glenny, quoted in Bruce Stave and Michele Palmer, Witnesses to Nuremberg: An Oral History of American Participants at the War Crimes Trials (Toronto: Prentice Hall International, 1998), 43.]

[23] Robert Ley (1890-1945) was leader of the German Labor Front from 1933 to 1945.

[24] Hermann Göring (1893-1946), *Reichsmarschal*, commander of the *Luftwaffe*, president of the Reichstag, and plenipotentiary of the Four Year Plan, was until 1942 the most powerful personality in Germany after Hitler. At Nuremberg he was the highest ranking Nazi.

Towards the end of November 1945 they constructed an ingenious lighting system for the cells. In front of the cover for the food opening they attached wire meshing **[page 9]** and fixed a hook to it on which they hung a horizontal lamp with a simple shade. When dinner was brought the contraption could be removed and then replaced. There was bright light until 8 p.m. and then they reduced the intensity with the help of a resistor. It was still light enough to read and I used to read in bed until 10 p.m. in order to get really tired. Even then you could not sleep well because the sentries had orders to wake you if you moved from the light and thus prevented them from seeing your face. The nice sentries - and most of them were nice - found that they could turn the lamp to one side so that the light only shone partly into the cell. The sentry could see enough and the situation was bearable for the inmate.[25]

Every two or three days we were shaved by a German barber. At the same time, the cell was damp mopped by the German staff. Every day we walked for precisely one hour, which was strictly regulated. Later it was one hour twice a day. The solitary confinement prisoners, five or six at a time, were taken out together for their walk, each with his own guard. We could move freely around the courtyard, but we were not allowed to get closer than five meters to one another and talking was forbidden. The guards had been ordered to beat you with a club or shoot if you tried to escape.[26] We had been warned about this directive in writing. Every Tuesday there were hot showers or one could take a bath in the basement of the building. Once a week the laundry was collected, washed and if necessary, mended. If needed, felt boots and warm winter jackets could be obtained from German supplies; **[page 10]** trousers, shirts, undershirts, and long underwear came from American supplies.

---

[25] A number of guards later confided that they found the regulations unrealistic-- shining lights in sleeping faces, poking prisoners if they slept facing the wall, forcing them to keep their hands above the blankets, and prohibiting conversation. They had not strictly enforced them.

[26] Andrus confirmed that his guards had orders to shoot any prisoner attempting to escape, but he hoped it would never happen.

We were allowed to write one letter and two postcards each week; we received American prisoner of war forms on Sundays. Theoretically, we were allowed to receive any mail. Nonetheless, we Austrians did not have any mail connection with our relatives, because the mail service between Germany and Austria was only re-established on 15 April 1946. In December 1945 Father Sixtus initiated a temporary post office at the headquarters of the American occupation troops in Salzburg, to which our relatives could direct their correspondence. I received the first letter from my wife in February 1946 after I had been here for four months. It only worked well from April onward. During English captivity, however, I had only been allowed to write twice and received one letter during a period of four and a half months.

The American psychiatrists played a special role. They were lead by Dr. Goldensohn[27] who dressed like a major. They were obviously Jews. Goldensohn was a homosexual and was always accompanied by his "wife." They visited the main defendants and interesting witnesses and gathered material for their studies. They were especially interested in sexual life. It was said that Goldensohn was working on a book that he wanted to publish in America.[28] Fortunately, I was not interesting enough.

A Catholic and a Protestant army chaplain were in charge of the prisoners' spiritual needs. They were fundamentally different sorts of men, but they worked with similar methods. They wore the same American officer's uniforms with a Captain's badge and a cross on the collar. The Protestant minister, **[page 11]** Pastor Guericke [sic],[29] was of German descent, spoke broken German and

---

[27] Major Leon N. Goldensohn succeeded Major Douglas Kelly as prison psychiatrist after the first month of the trial.

[28] Rainer possibly mixed up Goldensohn with Dr. Gustav Gilbert, who assumed an unofficial role as a prison psychologist, and Major Kelley. Originally Gilbert (who was Jewish) and Kelley had planned to write a collaborative book so they frequently went around the prison together. Both published books separately. Gilbert's <u>Nuremberg Diary</u> came first, followed by Kelley's <u>22 Cells at Nuremberg</u>.

[29] Captain (later Major) Henry Gerecke was a portly 54-year-old Lutheran chaplain from

belonged to a sect of the Lutherans, which is the fourth largest among some 70 Protestant sects in the United States. The Lutherans run missions among the heathens in Africa and the Middle East; the Paster [Gerecke] practiced his ministry according to their style. At the beginning of December he visited me in my cell and was sad when I told him that I would remain a heathen.[30] But he was glad that I took his propaganda leaflets, which interested me, and he always brought new ones. He invited me to the Christmas service and I gladly accepted, because I knew from my former experience in prison that this was the only opportunity to talk to fellow prisoners. Moreover, I was interested in what he would say. Dr. Guericke [sic] was a man with a good and compassionate heart who took his job very seriously, only perhaps he was not always with it. Nevertheless, he could bring together a respectable congregation of good Protestant Christians.[31]

The Catholic priest was Father Sixtus. He was a Franciscan. His grandmother came from Upper Austria and his father was Irish. Before the war he had spent some time in Germany and Austria and had studied Christian philosophy with Professor Dempf.[32] He understood German well and spoke so fluently that he could also include complex ideas in his sermons. Afterwards one could discuss the content of the sermon with him. He had a youthful, fresh

---

St. Louis, Missouri, who spoke a rough German, which he had learned growing up. He had had considerable experience with prisoners as the director of prison work for the St. Louis City Mission. He clearly endeared himself to the defendants. In the spring of 1946 when a rumor circulated that Gerecke was about to leave because his time in the military had ended, all 21 defendants signed and sent a petition to Mrs. Gereck asking her to persuade her husband to stay. Gerecke remained, eventually walking with half the defendants to the gallows.

[30] Rainer had been raised a Protestant, however.

[31] Gerecke and Sixtus held services in a chapel made from two cells where the intervening wall had been knocked down. Army blankets covered the concrete walls; the altar was a crate, also covered with a blanket. In one corner there was a wooden crucifix while another corner had a small, well used organ.

[32] Alois Dempf (1891-1982), an Austrian philosopher who opposed National Socialism, taught at universities in Vienna and Munich. In his work he attempted to synthesize anthropology, sociology, and philosophy.

appearance, and always wore an elegant uniform. Before Christmas 1945 he came into my cell for the first time, delivered greetings from the Austrians in the witnesses' wing and gave me the temporary postal address in Salzburg. I thought him to be an officer until he said he was a priest. He looked after the prisoners well and especially **[page 12]** liked the Austrians, perhaps because of his origins. Indeed thanks to his intervention Uiberreither and I were transferred from solitary confinement to the witnesses' wing on 4 January 1946.

Among the Americans in Nuremberg there were two points of view. One group wanted to condemn completely everything that was Nazi. The main prosecutor, Jackson,[33] and the CIC (American secret intelligence service)[34] belonged to this group. The other group wanted to stick to more just and perhaps more political principles. They were defeated at Christmas 1945 by the more radical group, and their main proponent, the American deputy prosecutor,[35] went back to America. Sixtus was definitely in favor of the more moderate view and from then on often had difficulties with Colonel Andrus because of his support for the prisoners. Some thought that Sixtus was all hypocrisy and that in reality he was an agent of the American secret service. I do not think so, but I believe him to be a clever exponent of the Catholic Church of America. I think he has some

---

[33] Robert Jackson (1892-1954), the head of the US prosecution team, had a distinguished legal and public career, including terms as Solicitor General and Attorney General. In 1941 President Roosevelt appointed him to the US Supreme Court. After the trial he returned to the Supreme Court, serving until his death in 1954 at age 62.

[34] The USA's Counter Intelligence Corps.

[35] This reference is unclear. Rainer may have been referring to Colonel Robert G. Storey, Jackson's deputy as Executive Trial Counsel. There had been differences between Storey and Colonel John H. Amen over whether to rely on documents (Storey) or witnesses (Amen) in the courtroom. Jackson's own position emphasized documents. Storey's departure in January 1946, however, was by a pre-trial arrangement with Jackson.

Alternatively, Rainer may have meant General Bill Donovan, the head of the Office of Strategic Services and initially one of Jackson's deputies. The two men had a major difference of approach and Donovan left after the reading of the indictments.

Rainer may also have confused this with another problem. Jackson had a raft of US lawyers of mixed talents; most were civilians in uniform. Once they acquired enough service for a discharge they would leave, often in the middle of a prosecution. By January 1946 Jackson had only 13 of his original 150 lawyers.

connection with Cardinal Spellman.[36] His ministry was very successful. Many influential members of the Party and especially of the SS joined his Church, e.g. *Reichsschatzmeister* (Reich Treasurer) and *SS-Oberstgruppenführer* (General) Schwarz,[37] *Reichsleiter* and *SS-Obergruppenführer* (Lieutenant General) Amann,[38] *Reichsarzt* (Chief Physician) of the *Waffen-SS* and *SS-Obergruppenführer* Dr. Karl Gebhardt [sic],[39] Reich Minister Dr. Frank, *SS-Obergruppenführer* Kaltenbrunner,[40] *SS-Obergruppenführer* Von-dem-Bach-Zelewski,[41] *SS-Brigadeführer* (Brigadier General) Schellenberg[42] and nearly all the members of the Reich Security Main Office.[43] Papen[44] and Seyss-Inquart[45] had not left the

---

[36] Francis J. Spellman (1889-1967), archbishop of New York since 1939 and a cardinal after February 1946, argued that there was a close association of freedom with Christian principles. During the war he had identified the cause of the allies (excluding Russia) with Christian civilization.

[37] Franz Xaver Schwarz (1875-1947) was the treasurer of the NSDAP from 1925 until 1945. He died in an internment camp near Regensburg.

[38] Max Amann (1891-1957), a war time comrade of Hitler, joined the NSDAP immediately upon its founding as member #3. He built the Eher Press into the Nazi's main publishing house and served as Hitler's personal banker. After 1933 he amalgamated the German and Nazi presses until they became the same. By 1942 he controlled 80% of all newspapers and had an enormous income. After the war his property was confiscated and he died in poverty.

[39] Karl Gebhart, born in Upper Bavaria in either 1897 or 1898, was on very close terms with Himmler, serving as his adviser. He was also head of the German Red Cross.

[40] Ernst Kaltenbrunner (1903-1946), a leading member of the Austrian SS, succeeded Reinhard Heydrich as chief of the Reich Security Main Office (RSHA) in January 1943.

[41] Erich von dem Bach-Zelewski (1899-1972) was responsible for anti-partisan warfare on the eastern front and commanded the German units which crushed the Warsaw uprising in the summer of 1944. At Nuremberg he testified on behalf of the prosecution. In and out of prison after the war he eventually received a life sentence.

[42] Walter Schellenberg (1910-1952), a protégé of Heinrich Himmler, played a major role in creating the Reich Security Main Office. In 1941 he became head of espionage services (Amt VI) and was involved in several daring undercover operations, including a failed attempt to kidnap the Duke and Duchess of Windsor from Lisbon. At war's end he expedited Himmler's plans for a separate surrender to the West. Sentenced to six years in prison in 1949, he received a pardon in 1950.

[43] This office, the *Reichssicherheitshauptamt*, established in September 1939, was a subsidiary organization of the SS, merging the Security Service (SD), the Gestapo, and the criminal police. Its goal was to fight all enemies of the Reich.

Church. The ministrants[46] were Papen, General Warlimont[47] of the OKW [*Oberkommando der Wehrmacht*] and *U-Boot-Oberleutnant* (Submarine Lieutenant) Heissig [sic],[48] who was a witness **[page 13]** against Dönitz.[49] Father Sixtus was known to rouse opportunistic, political, or religious feelings. If the Americans only learned to play this time, they would win over masses of Germans who readily grasp every hand stretched out to them, as they are outcasts of the world. Father Sixtus was always very kind to me. He brought me some interesting books about modern Christian philosophy and existentialism according to Kierkegaard[50] and Heidegger.[51] He did not try to convert me.

---

[44] Franz von Papen (1879-1969), a leading Catholic politician, was German chancellor in 1932 and Hitler's deputy chancellor from 1933 to 1934. He later served as German minister in Vienna and then went to Turkey as ambassador from 1939 to 1945. Acquitted at Nuremberg he was later sentenced to 8 years imprisonment by a German court.

[45] Arthur Seyss-Inquart (1892-1946), a fellow Austrian and Rainer's colleague since 1936, played a key role in the 1938 *Anschluss* and served briefly as Austrian Chancellor. Later he was deputy to Hans Frank in Poland and then served as Reich commissioner in Holland from 1940 to 1945. Tried at Nuremberg, he was found guilty and executed. Rainer testified at the IMT on his behalf.

[46] Those who attended the priest conducting the mass.

[47] Walter Warlimont (1894-1976), a veteran of the First World War, studied in the USA and served as military attaché in France. He was one of the few German officers with practical overseas experience and a realistic world view. From 1939 he served as deputy chief of *Wehrmacht* Operations. Sentenced to life imprisonment in the OKW (High Command of the Armed Forces) 1948 trial he was amnestied in 1957.

[48] Peter Joseph Heisig, born in 1921 in Breslau, was a submarine officer. He was called to Nuremberg as a prosecution witness against Admiral Dönitz regarding the murder of allied seamen. He complained to Andrus that the others ostracized him because he was neither a Nazi nor a militarist. Subsequently he left Nuremberg in February 1946 for a civilian internment camp.

[49] Karl Dönitz (1891-1980) was responsible for developing and deploying the German submarine fleet. In 1943 he succeeded Admiral Erich Raeder as head of the German navy and upon Hitler's death, became Chancellor. He subsequently surrendered the Third Reich unconditionally to the Allies in May 1945. Tried by the IMT, he was found guilty and sentenced to ten years in prison.

[50] Soren Kierkegaard (1813-1855) was a Danish philosopher. His concept of man as an isolated individual before God is considered a foundation of Existentialism.

[51] Martin Heidegger (1889-1976), the German philosopher, is often considered the chief exponent of Existentialism.

The German staff came from prisoner of war camps and consisted of Germans from the Reich and Austrians. It was forbidden for us to speak of anything other than what directly pertained to their work. They had chosen those people who were known to be sympathetic to Social Democracy or to a Christian party. Nevertheless, a relatively friendly atmosphere developed. Once when a transport of popular generals like Brauchitsch[52] and Kesselring[53] left, the prisoners of war helped carry the luggage and shook hands on leaving. Consequently, Andrus locked up all those involved for 24 hours and forbade helping and shaking hands. In the spring of 1946 the prisoners of war were given the status of civilian employees. They were paid and had holidays. Some old men were allowed to go home.

At the beginning of 1946, the rumor spread among the Americans that units of the SS under the command of Skorzeny[54] had come near Nuremberg in order to free the prisoners. Tanks were placed around the complex, barricades of sandbags were erected at all entrances and corners, each guard **[page 14]** was

---

[52] Walter von Brauchitsch (1881-1948) was commander in chief of the German army from 1938 to 1941. He retired after the first set backs on the eastern front. Arrested at the end of the war he died while in a British camp awaiting trial.

[53] Albert Kesselring (1885-1960) was field marshal of the air force and commander in chief of German troops in Italy from 1941 to 1945. A British military court sentenced him to death for the execution of hostages but then commuted the sentence to life imprisonment. He was released due to ill health in 1952.

[54] Otto Skorzeny (1908-1975), born in Vienna, a colonel in the SS, rose to prominence with his daring 1943 rescue of Mussolini. Later he played a major role in the October 1944 arrest of Miklos Horthy, the Hungarian head of state. He was held at Nuremberg as a possible prosecution witness although he never testified. Tried by an American tribunal in Dachau in 1947 he was acquitted. He later fled from an internment camp and settled in Spain where he established a prosperous cement business.

The rumor was actually not about Skorzeny, but about SS and *Wehrmacht* troops interned in camps a few miles away. Supposedly, they planned a mass escape with the intent of attacking the Nuremberg jail. Consequently, the US army strengthened its security, placing machine guns in the courthouse and jail, moved in tank units, and established roadblocks. Intelligence sources also received information that sometime between 6 and 20 February seven men dressed in Allied uniforms and carrying forged credentials would attempt to disrupt the trial, possibly by assassinating judges and prosecutors. Nothing happened but the discovery of dynamite on railroad tracks at nearby Furth on 30 January kept officials on maximum alert.

assigned an alarm post marked with a number, and in the witnesses' wing they built an armored post for machine guns on a corridor bridge on the second floor. The Americans worked clumsily in the presence of the competent German generals. Every now and then there were alarm drills. The funny thing was that Skorzeny had been imprisoned in the cell block since October, and had watched all the measures taken for his defeat from the witness's wing. He even drew the Americans' attention to the fact that he was there, but this was thought to be a tactical ploy.

Often American visitors came, groups of officers or soldiers, Congressmen, union leaders, journalists and women, among them the wife and daughter of the American Commander in Chief MacNarney [sic].[55] Famous guests were shown around by Andrus himself, and interesting inmates were either introduced personally or at least their name plates on the door were pointed out. Most of us avoided this show business. One way was to go to the toilet whenever a visitor approached. Andrus was very anxious about his reputation as a prison director. The defendant Streicher had declared at court how he had been abused and tortured during his interrogation. The army newspaper Stars and Stripes reported on this without saying where it had happened.[56] In an extremely excited manner, Andrus arrived and made a statement that this had not happened in his prison. This was right. The treatment in Nuremberg was good.

---

[55] Joseph T. McNarney succeeded Dwight Eisenhower in November 1945, taking over all the jobs held by Ike: commander of US forces in the European Theater, commander-in-chief of US occupation forces in Germany, and US representative on the Allied Control Council for Germany. McNarney had been Einsenhower's deputy chief of staff.

[56] During his testimony Julius Streicher claimed, "During my internment I have been treated in the way the Gestapo has been accused of acting... I have been beaten and chained to the floor with an iron chain. I have been forced to kiss the feet of Negroes. People spit into my face and open mouth. When I asked for water I was ordered to drink from the latrine." His charges were stricken from the record as irrelevant. ["GIs Beat Me, Gestapo-Style, Steicher Says," Stars and Stripes, 27 April 1946.]

In the witnesses' wing, where I stayed from 4 January to 21 June 1946,[57] the doors to the cells were open and the inmates **[page 15]** could move about freely. Only the second floor was closed off and divided into two separate parts. In one part there were about ten witnesses of the prosecuting counsel, who for some reason were kept apart from the other witnesses before they gave their evidence before the court. Among them there were Bach-Zelewski, Schellenberg, Colonel General Blaskowitz,[58] General Rötiger [sic],[59] who had worked as chief of staff under Kesselring and Vietinghof-Scheel,[60] *Brigadeführer* Rohde [sic],[61] Chief of the Command Staff SS (*Kommandostabes-Reichsführer SS*) etc. In the other part there were the women, among them Himmler's wife and daughter,[62] Frau Streicher,[63] the *Führer*'s secretary Wolf,[64] the secretaries of Frank, Hess and

---

[57] Prior to this time Rainer was kept in solitary confinement. His separation, as for all witnesses, was to prevent any coordination or collaboration which might bias his interrogation.

[58] Johannes Blaskowitz (1883-1948) prepared the plan of attack on Poland and commanded the German 8th Army. He then became commander in chief of the army of occupation until dismissed because of his protests against SS brutalities and excesses. He committed suicide in 1948 shortly before the start of his trial as a war criminal.

[59] Hans Röttiger, from Hamburg, was chief of the General Staff in Army Group Southwest (Italy). He served under Albert Kesselring and Heinrich Vietinghof-Scheel.

[60] Heinrich Vietinghof-Scheel, born in Mainz in 1887, served with distinction in the West, the Balkans, and on the Russian front and ended the war as commander of Army Group Southwest. His motto was, "I lead from the front."

[61] Ernst Rode, born 9 August 1894, assumed the post as chief of the Command Staff of the *Reichsführer-SS* in the summer of 1943. His special responsibility was to furnish the forces necessary for antipartisan warfare. His last rank was Major General of the Police and *Waffen-SS*.

[62] Margarete (Marga) Boden Himmler was the daughter of a German landowner from West Prussia. After a career as a nurse and a first marriage she married Himmler in July 1928. She and Heinrich eventually drifted apart. They had one daughter Gudrun.

[63] Adele Streicher, born in 1906 in Magdeburg, was an attractive, charming blond, but like Streicher, an unrelenting and vocal anti-Semite. Some 20 years younger than Streicher, she worked as his secretary from 1941 to 1945.

[64] Johanna Wolf, born 1 June 1900, was Hitler's chief private secretary from January 1930 to April 1945. She never married but lived on until at least her 80th birthday. Hitler's other secretaries were Christa Schroeder, Gerda (Dara) Christian, and Gertrud Junge.

Ribbentrop and others.[65] They were guarded very attentively by American nurses. All the other inmates were distributed on the lower two floors. Witnesses for the prosecution, witnesses for the defense and future defendants were mixed together. Usually you stayed in solitary confinement until you were interrogated and then you joined the rest. This is general American practice, as the court thinks it natural that the witnesses talk among themselves. In the course of time nearly all the leading personalities of the Party, the state and the military passed through the witnesses' wing. There were strange encounters. I was together with the generals Halder[66] and Falkenhausen,[67] who had both been in the KZ[68] because of a mutiny and who complained to Andrus that they had been treated better in the German prison. Dr. Brand [sic],[69] the physician to the *Führer*, had his cell near *Obergruppenführer* Berger,[70] who as president of a war tribunal **[page 16]** had sentenced him to death for cowardice at the end of the war. Now they could discuss the case in peace. The atmosphere among the inmates was polite and friendly despite their differing views. Their common fate made the differences

---

[65] Helena Kraffczyk was secretary to Hans Frank; Hildegarde Fath, Ingeborg Speer, and Laura Schroedl to Rudolf Hess; Margaret Blank to Joachim Ribbentrop; and Hildegarde Brüninghoff to Robert Ley.

[66] Franz Halder (1884-1972), Hitler's Chief of the Army General Staff on the eve of the war, eventually clashed with Hitler over policy. This led to his transfer to the reserves in September 1942. Suspected of involvement in the July 1944 assassination attempt on Hitler, he was imprisoned until the war's end.

[67] Alexander Freiherr von Falkenhausen (1878-1966) was military governor of Belgium and Northern France. He opposed the Nazi excesses and sought to protect the population from the worst of the occupation. Imprisoned for his part in the 1944 assassination attempt on Hitler he was saved by US troops just before his execution. Although tried by the Belgians for war crimes and sentenced to 12 years he was released because of his anti-Hitler record.

[68] *Konzentrationslager* or concentration camp.

[69] Karl Brandt (1904-1948), one of Hitler's personal physicians, vied with Theodor Morell for the *Führer*'s favors. In 1942 he became Reich Commissioner for Sanitation and Health until Hitler sacked him in October 1944. Saved from Nazi execution by Himmler and Speer he was convicted after the war for criminal experiments on humans and executed.

[70] Gottlob Berger (1896-1975) had helped Himmler organize the *Waffen-SS*, served in the SS Main Office, and after 1944 was responsible for POW affairs.

seem less important. Often they voiced the wish that they should have organized such meetings earlier, so that they could have had a better relationship and many a quarrel might have been avoided.

Until May 1946 everybody in the witnesses' wing had his own cell. The light was still on the ceiling and there were still real tables and chairs. Even though it was forbidden, everybody had their nails and clothes-line and American blankets as wall covers. You could take anything you needed from your cases. Every week there was a new razor blade, which you were allowed to keep for shaving. You kept the dishes and washed them with hot water in huge pots. You kept the building and cells clean, although this became a job for the younger men. In the mornings and afternoons we each took a walk for one hour with companions of our choice. The daily routine was the following: get up at 7 a.m., breakfast at 7.15, lunch at noon, dinner at 6 p.m. By 10 p.m. everybody had to be in their cells with lights out. A sergeant accompanied by two or three sentries was responsible for guarding us. Bridge and skat[71] clubs were formed and there were many English courses and evening lectures.[72] From May 1946 onward, huge crowds of witnesses for the accused organizations and groups arrived. The special group of men on the second floor was dispersed, and the last 18 individual witnesses, of which I was one, were segregated there. All the other witnesses were crammed together into the cells in threes and fours. After the witnesses had been at court, they were taken to the internment camps at Hers-**[page 17]** bruck, Langwasser or Dachau.[73]

[71] A three handed card game popular in Germany.

[72] Although the witnesses engaged in evening activities the main defendants were isolated from each other except at church. Only after receiving their verdicts did the defendants have more freedom. Andrus converted an unoccupied cell into a club room and stocked it with playing cards, chess sets, and other games. Each defendant could have two parties to which he could invite three other defendants. The men rarely stopped talking, leaving the games untouched.

[73] Hersbruck near Nuremberg housed Civilian Internment Enclosure #4. Langwasser, just north of Nuremberg, had been Stalag XIIID but after the war it became a detention camp as Prisoner of War Enclosure (PWE) #29. At one time Langwasser held twenty thousand hardened SS veterans. Dachau was the Nazis' first concentration camp, dating from the spring of 1933.

Not all the witnesses were imprisoned. A group of men who were apparently not considered to be war criminals, were kept under minimal security in an inn.[74] Among them were the *Führer*'s private photographer, Professor Hofmann [sic],[75] and Schuschnig's[76] [sic] Chief of Police, Dr. Skubl.[77] Witnesses who were believed to be definite enemies of the Nazis were freely accommodated in hotel rooms.

I would add that every week they distributed tobacco. At first there were German cigars and German tobacco, then there was American tobacco, sometimes a lot, sometimes a little. During the court session the chief defendants received an allowance of American so-called A-, B-, or C-parcels, which contained chocolate, cheese, cookies, tobacco, chewing gum, etc.

In the middle of November 1945 I was taken through the wooden corridor to the Palace of Justice for the first interrogation.[78] An American Colonel appeared with an interpreter and a man with a dictating machine. The interpreter told me to raise my right hand, the Colonel said something in English, and I was taken under oath without knowing whether I was to be interrogated as a defendant or as a witness. Then the colonel asked me about my discussions with Kesselring

---

[74] The IMT operated the Witness House, a requisitioned dwelling at Novalis Strasse 24, Nuremberg-Erlenstegen. Countess Ingeborg Kalnoky, a German married to a Hungarian, served as the hostess.

[75] Heinrich Hoffman (1885-1957) was the official photographer of Hitler and the Nazi party. An intimate associate with Hitler from the beginning of his political career in 1919, he retained the *Führer*'s trust until the end. After the war Hoffman was sentenced to hard labor and a loss of property as a Nazi beneficiary.

[76] Kurt von Schuschnigg (1897-1977), the Austrian chancellor from 1934 to 1938, imprisoned after the 1938 *Anschluss,* subsequently emigrated to the United States where he became a political science professor at St. Louis University and a naturalized US citizen.

[77] Michael Skubl was the Austrian State Secretary for Security who loyally served both chancellors Engelburt Dollfuss and his successor Schuschnigg.

[78] Rainer was interrogated three times by the Americans in November 1945. His interrogator was Colonel Curtis L. Williams while the interpreter was Alfred H. Booth. Transcripts of the three interrogations are located at the National Archives and Records Administration (NARA), College Park, Maryland, and the Imperial War Museum, London.

concerning the partisan fight and with Sauckel[79] about procuring labor. He was accurately informed that I had protested against Kesselring's order concerning the fight against the partisans, that it had been hard for me to give voice to my strong disapproval of the collective measures, that Kesselring had opposed my long term amnesty and that I did not permit forcible methods of procuring labor in my districts. He could have obtained this **[page 18]** information only from *Obergruppenführer* Wolff[80] who had been in Nuremberg before me and knew these circumstances. The Colonel now wanted to get detailed information as to how Kesselring and Sauckel proceeded in other districts and what cruelties and instances of violence occurred there. I could only declare truthfully that Kesselring and Sauckel had been influenced by me, that Kesselring followed my example later on and also came out with a major amnesty,[81] and that events in other districts were unknown to me as I was fully preoccupied with my own concerns. The Colonel was very dissatisfied, became more and more unfriendly and loud, and since I firmly refused to give evidence about things I knew nothing about, the hearing ended. It taught me no respect for American methods. The hearing was typed on the spot by the court recorder. I have never seen nor signed the minutes.

One week later they came for me again and I was interrogated about Austria. Again the colonel started in quite a friendly manner, giving me to feel

---

[79] Fritz Sauckel (1894-1946), plenipotentiary general for labor mobilization from 1942 to 1945, had responsibility for forced labor in the Reich.

[80] Karl Wolff (1900-1985) was head of Himmler's personal staff and his adjutant until 1943 when Himmler dismissed him because he divorced his wife. Sent then as military governor of Northern Italy, Wolff negotiated an early surrender of that region, a consideration which meant lenient treatment after the war. Not until the aftermath of the Adolf Eichmann trial in 1961was he charged and sentenced for complicity in the Final Solution.

[81] In September 1943 Rainer offered an amnesty to all Bolsheviks who through "error, seduction, or compulsion" had joined the partisans. They could return home to live peacefully with their families without fear of punishment, but they had to abide by German law. In his Nuremberg interrogation Rainer does not mention an amnesty by Kesselring, but he does report that his (Rainer's) amnesty was "practically approved by Kesselring and by [Karl] Wolff."

that he was quite well-informed about the fact that I had favored a moderate and political line and had fought against the violent and terrorist methods of others. Then, I was supposed to give evidence against Seyss, which was not possible, since I have been even more radical than Seyss. I, therefore, in truth, exonerated Seyss, and took the blame upon myself, which again incensed the Colonel. On the same afternoon I had my third and last interrogation. It dealt with a short report about the takeover on 11 March 1938, which I had delivered to Bürkel [sic][82] in 1939 **[page 19]** and a copy of which I had sent to Seyss with an accompanying letter.[83] Both had been found in the papers of Seyss. The reason for the report was Bürckel's attempt to discredit Seyss with the *Führer* and overthrow him on account of his seeming hesitation on 11 March 1938. I thought this indecent and described the events in such a way as to exonerate Seyss. Now the report was an important piece of evidence for the prosecution and I was to confirm its authenticity and correctness. I confirmed the authenticity. As to the correctness I stated my reservation that the report was colored by a certain bias. In truth certain actions were not to be ascribed to Seyss, but to me. Later on I also found some errors which had escaped me. My declarations were taken into the minutes which I never saw and never signed, however. It was indicative of the prosecution's method that in Court it was asserted I had confirmed the authenticity and the correctness of the contents while my stated reservations were suppressed.

The strange manner of interrogation was part of the American method as I learned later in the witnesses' wing. They tried to win witnesses for the prosecution from the circles of leading National Socialists. According to Anglo-

---

[82] Josef Bürckel (1895-1944) began his Nazi career as *Gauleiter* in the Rheinpfalz. In 1935 he was Reich Commissioner in charge of the successful reincorporation of the Saar. After the 1938 *Anschluss* he served as Reich Commissioner of Austria, charged with the task of incorporating the country into the Reich. From 1939 to 1940 he was *Gauleiter* of Vienna while simultaneously serving as *Gauleiter* of Saarpfalz (renamed Gau Westmark), a post he held until his suicide in September 1944.

[83] Copies of Rainer's correspondence with Bürckel and Seyss-Inquart, plus his "Report on the events in the NSDAP of Austria since the beginning of the last stage of battle until the seizure of power on the 11th March 1938" are found in the Nuremberg trial records as Document 812-PS.

Saxon law, witnesses for the prosecution go unpunished, even if they were accomplices of the defendant, if they testify against him in Court. They obviously counted on the attractiveness of this method, and they did not go wrong in many cases, as was seen during the trial. Only a few reliable witnesses miscalculated, **[page 20]** for after testifying in court they were accused of other actions or they were extradited. I have the impression, nevertheless, that in this way many witnesses saved their skins.

The principal defendants and a number of other leading personalities had been interned after the surrender in a large hotel in Mondorf in Luxembourg.[84] There, I was told, they were still treated as captured statesmen and generals had been treated. As I was told by one defense counsel, many of them handed over so-called "justification papers" to the CIC, in which they reported honestly and plainly about the events in the area of their competence. Indeed, they expected a prosecution of concrete war crimes according to The Hague Convention,[85] but not a prosecution of the whole system since the founding of the Nazi movement and on the basis of an after the fact law. The CIC confirmed this belief to them and thus received materials in hand which were extremely useful for the prosecution as was shown in the course of the trial. From Mondorf the future defendants were taken to Nuremberg where they stayed first in the Grand Hotel. Meanwhile the Palace of Justice was modified with a wing for cells. On its completion they were taken to prison there. Most of the witnesses stayed at first in the American CIC Interrogation Center Oberursel[86] from where they were taken to camps or directly to Nuremberg. Witnesses, themselves scheduled for trial or extradition, ended up

---

[84] Twelve of the defendants (plus others, some of whom would be witnesses) were inmates of "Ashcan," the Palace Hotel, Mondorf-les Bain, Luxembourg, where they remained until moved to Nuremberg in August 1945.

[85] The Hague Conventions Respecting the Laws and Customs of War on Land, dating from 1899 and 1907, had codified the laws and customs of war. They were signed by more than 40 states.

[86] Oberursel was near Frankfurt am Main.

finally in Dachau, the collecting camp for all "War Criminals" of the American zone.

[page 21] The defendants received the written charges exactly one month before the beginning of the main proceedings. I read them later on. They were relatively short, in any case shorter than the "Bluebook"[87] in our Ljubljana trial. They had a general part, a very short personal section on each of the defendants, and at the end the points of indictment against the six accused organizations whose criminal character was to be determined in connection with the judgment against the 22 principal defendants.[88] Originally there was a 23rd defendant, Krupp von Bohlen;[89] he was dropped because of an alleged illness. Dr. Ley, the 24th chief defendant, was deleted because of his suicide. Bormann[90] was

---

[87] When the Yugoslavs tried Rainer in July 1947 the indictments against him and his associates were contained in a 114-page book with a blue cover.

[88] The 22 defendants (with Nuremberg prisoner number) were: (1) Karl Dönitz (31 G 350024), grand admiral, head of the German fleet, supreme commander of the German armed forces and Hitler's successor; (2) Hans Frank (31 G 350010), Governor-General of Poland; (3) Wilhelm Frick (31 G 350006), Interior Minister and Reich Protector for Bohemia/Moravia; (4) Hans Fritzsche (31 G 350146), chief of broadcasting in the Propaganda Ministry; (5) Walther Funk (31 G 350044), head of the Reichsbank and Economics Minister; (6) Hermann Göring (31 G 350013), head of the Luftwaffe and designated successor to Hitler; (7) Rudolf Hess (31 G 350125), Hitler's deputy; (8) Alfred Jodl (31 G 350026), head of planning for the High Command, general, and chief of the German Armed Forces; (9) Ernst Kaltenbrunner (31 G 350082), chief of the Reich Security Main Office; (10) Wilhelm Keitel (31 G 350003), chief of the High Command of the German Armed Forces; (11) Robert Ley, head of the German Labor Front; (12) Constantin von Neurath (31 G 350114), former Foreign Minister and Reich Protector of Czechoslovakia; (13) Franz von Papen (31 G 350018), Vice Chancellor and ambassador; (14) Erich Raeder (31 G 350147), navy commander in chief; (15) Joachim von Ribbentrop (31 G 350052), Minister of Foreign Affairs; (16) Alfred Rosenberg (31 G 350042), Reich Minister for the Eastern Occupied Territories; (17) Fritz Sauckel, General Plenipotentiary for the Mobilization of Labor; (18) Hjalmar Schacht (31 G 350126), Finance Minister; (19) Baldur von Schirach (31 G 350085), Hitler Youth Leader; (20) Arthur Seyss-Inquart (31 G 350001), governor of the Netherlands; (21) Albert Speer (31 G 350037), Munitions Minister; and (22) Julius Steicher (31 G 350049), editor of Der Stürmer and *Gauleiter* of Franconia

[89] Gustav Krupp von Bohlen und Halbach (1870-1950) was the German arms manufacturer and Hitler's leader of the Reich Estate of German Industry. Although indicted, he was declared incapable of standing trial because of his age and health.

[90] Martin Bormann (1900-1945), head of the party chancellery and secretary to Hitler, was one of the closest *Führer* confidants and one of the most powerful men in Germany. He disappeared in 1945, but was tried and sentenced to death in absentia. In 1973 a West German

prosecuted since his death was apparently not confirmed. Hitler was not prosecuted since his death was apparently confirmed.[91] In reality, the reason might have been that his indictment would have been the best exoneration for the rest. The crimes were arranged according to the four main categories of the London Charter:[92] 1. Conspiracy against world peace, 2. Waging a war of aggression, 3. Crimes against the customs and practices of war, 4. Crimes against humanity. The accused organizations were the Reich government,[93] the General Staff,[94] the corps of Political Leaders,[95] the SS,[96] the SA,[97] the Gestapo,[98] and the SD.[99]

I think the Charter was written by the USA, Great Britain and USSR in July 1945. France later signed it. These four states were called the signatories of

---

court formally pronounced him dead.

[91] Although Hitler's death was not confirmed, the reason he was not tried in absentia was so other defendants could not defer to him and claim they were only following his orders.

[92] The London Charter (also called the London Agreement), signed 8 August 1945 by France, the Soviet Union, the United Kingdom, and the USA, and acceded to by the 19 countries that comprised the United Nations War Crimes Commission, established the basis for prosecuting those accused of committing atrocities during the war. It defined the acts considered war crimes: crimes against peace, war crimes, and crimes against humanity. The three categories of crimes were extended into four indictment counts: (1) the common plan or conspiracy; (2) crimes against peace; (3) war crimes; and (4) crimes against humanity. Rainer has erred slightly in his description of the four main crime categories.

[93] The Reich Cabinet.

[94] The high command of the German armed forces.

[95] The leaders of the NSDAP.

[96] *Die Schutzstaffeln der NSDAP*, the SS or Defense Squads, began as a small group entrusted with the personal safety of Hitler. Under Himmler it became the largest police, intelligence, and national security agency in the Third Reich.

[97] The paramilitary SA, *Die Sturmabteilung der NSDAP*, or the Brown Shirts, was the "striking" arm of the Nazi party in the years before Hitler came to power.

[98] *Die Geheime Staatspolizei*, the secret police, was created in the spring 1933 under Göring. After Himmler took over as leader its membership grew to over 30,000.

[99] *Der Sicherheitsdienst*, the internal security service within the SS, was founded in 1931 to identify political enemies and dissenters.

the London Charter. The American Supreme Court Judge Jackson, who subsequently became the chief prosecutor, had drawn up the Charter. According to the Charter the International Commission for the Assessment of War Crimes[100] was identical with the prosecuting authority. The Commission appointed the law court and issued the order of proceedings. It made all individual decisions, **[page 22]** except those concerning the course of the trial, which were made by the Court itself. The Charter contained the formal and material regulations for sentencing all war criminals. From this we can deduce that the prosecutor was at the same time legislator, executive, court of preliminary inquiry, court of inquiry and prosecution authority. The right of amnesty was vested in the Interallied Control Council[101] formed by the four signatory powers. The law court consisted of representatives of the four signatory states, as did the commission of the prosecution. The victorious powers were thus the supreme judicial authority, the judge, and the court of preliminary inquiry, as well as providing the counsel for the prosecution. This was not a neutral institution, the way international legal practices had appeared without exception up to now. According to the Charter, the content of all official statements of the four signatory powers was to be regarded as fully valid proof beyond which no further inquiries were allowed. Thus, in the presentation of evidence the decisive advantage was also conceded to the four signatory victorious powers. The merest assertion on their part had to be taken as fully proven. With all these regulations the standards of an objective judgment do not seem to me to have been maintained.

The defendants could choose their lawyers themselves from a list of permitted attorneys.[102] There were no National Socialists among them.[103] The

---

[100] The United Nations War Crimes Commission.

[101] The Allied Control Council.

[102] The defense counsels included: Friedrich Bergold (Martin Bormann); Rudolf Dix (Hjalmar Schacht); Franz Exner (Alfred Jodl); Hans Flächsner (Albert Speer); Otto Freiherr von Lüdinghausen (Constantin von Neurath); Heinz Fritz (Hans Fritzsche); Martin Horn (Joachim von Ribbentrop from 5 January 1946); Kurt Kauffmann (Ernst Kaltenbrunner); Otto Kranzbühler (Karl

lawyers were paid by the court.[104] They were given private lodgings in Nuremberg and help in procuring food for themselves and their staff. They were allowed to confer with the defendants freely and without supervision. There was only one guard present, who in most cases did not know German and was usually asleep. The defense lawyers had meetings among themselves. **[page 23]** Also the defendants were allowed to confer alone and in the presence of their lawyers. The lawyers were assured of the court's protection in exercising their duties. Once during the session when the communist newspaper of Nuremberg started an attack on some of the defense lawyers, the President of the Tribunal, Lord Judge Lawrence,[105] issued another declaration of protection.[106]

Dönitz); Egon Kubuschok (Franz von Papen; Reich Cabinet); Hanns Marx (Julius Streicher); Otto Nelte (Wilhelm Keitel); Otto Pannenbecker (Wilhelm Frick); Gunther von Rohrscheidt (Rudolf Hess to 5 February 1946); Fritz Sauter (Joachim von Ribbentrop to 6 January 1946; also Walther Funk and Baldur von Schirach); Alfred Seidl (Hess from 5 February 1946; Hans Frank); Robert Servatius (Fritz Sauckel; Leadership Corps of Nazi Party); Walter Siemers (Erich Raeder); Otto Stahmer (Hermann Göring); Gustav Steinbauer (Arthur Seyss-Inquart); and Alfred Thoma (Alfred Rosenberg).

[103] While most of the counsel for the defendants had not been Nazi party members, several had in fact belonged to the party: Kurt Kauffmann; Hans Marx joined in 1933 but was dismissed in 1935; Otto Nelte joined in 1933, then had his membership declared invalid in 1935, only to have it restored in 1938; Fritz Sauter from 1935 to 1940, although he was subsequently excluded because he defended Jews and Communists; and Alfred Seidl from 1937 to 1945. In addition several associate counsels had also belonged to the party: Werner Bross; George Froschmann; Hans Gawlik; Willi Heim; Josef Kössl; Günther Lummert; Hans Pribilla; and Joseph Weisgerber.

[104] The US Army newspaper, Stars and Stripes, reported that the defense lawyers received their fees from the defendant's blocked bank accounts. For example, thirteen of the defendants held more than 3,000,000 marks in Bavarian banks alone. Frick had the largest account of 1.23 million marks while Streicher was second with 1.087 million marks.

[105] Geoffrey Lawrence of the United Kingdom had had a distinguished legal career, most recently as Judge of the High Court of Justice, King's Bench, and then Lord Justice of Appeal. After the Nuremberg trial he was elevated to the peerage as Baron Oaksey. He died in 1971.

[106] Lawrence twice made declarations in court concerning the protection of defense counsel, first on 5 March and then on 31 August 1946. On the second occasion, Lawrence announced that the Tribunal would protect counsel as long as the Tribunal was in session and that the Control Council should then protect them thereafter. He added further that they were performing an important public task in accordance with the high tradition of the legal profession; on behalf of the Tribunal, Lawrence thanked them for their assistance.

So far as they had not been destroyed, all German archives, collections of documents and records, war diaries, and other materials had fallen into the hands of the victors. They were fully at the disposition of the prosecution. The defense was expressly excluded from using them.[107] Thus they could not rely on German official documents. Foreign documents, which the prosecution amply used, were denied them [the defense] from the beginning. The secret archives of the victorious states concerning the background of the war were not opened at all. The use of German documents concerning breaches of international law by others, which, according to existing arrangements, had been sent every year in thick volumes to the International Arbitration Tribunal[108] at The Hague, was denied. Field Marshall Keitel[109] pointed out that a number of German offences against the Hague Convention were intentional reprisals in order to force the other side again to renounce its own breaches of international law. The court did not allow this evidence as only the German crimes, and not the actions of the victors, were the subject of the trial.[110] But as a war is known to be a two sided affair, the one-sided picture offered by the trial concerning the war's causes and the methods of waging the war, did not correspond to the truth. **[page 24]** An historically objective

---

[107] This statement is not accurate although the Germans certainly worked under handicapped conditions. Most German documents were held by the Allies, making it difficult for defense counsel to gain access, especially since there were no indexes nor any way of knowing document contents. The lawyers could not begin to prepare their cases until the indictments were served in October 1945 only one month before the trial began. Further, since the lawyers were in court by day they had only evenings and weekends to prepare. But the defense attorneys were provided secretarial and translation services plus office space, and they had virtually unlimited time to confer with their clients.

[108] Rainer probably meant the Permanent Court of Arbitration, founded in 1899, which became a foundation for the Permanent Court of International Justice established at the Hague in January 1922.

[109] Wilhelm Keitel (1882-1946) pursued an administrative career in the military, becoming Chief of Staff to the War Minister in 1935. Head of the OKW from its inception in 1938 he retained this post to the end and served as one of Hitler's loyal subordinates.

[110] This point refers to the *tu quoque* argument ("you were doing it too") which the Germans were forbidden to use.

examination, availing itself equally of the sources from both sides, will offer a different picture.

No attention was given to the fact that in many points the Hague Land Warfare Convention[111] [*Landkriegsordnung*] is obsolete and needed, or would have need of a supplement; for example, concerning the war at sea, the war in the air, the use of commandos, the partisan war, and so on. Violations of such outdated regulations committed by both sides should not legally be charged to one side. Yet this occurred, with a single exception, which was accomplished by Admiral Dönitz's lawyer, Navy Judge (*Marinerichter*) Dr. Kranzbühler.[112] Among other things Dönitz was accused of unrestricted submarine warfare, which is actually against international law according to the Hague statute. Dr. Kranzbühler succeeded in obtaining written evidence from the American Admiral Nimitz in which he stated that America and also England waged unrestricted submarine war from the beginning. Dönitz was acquitted on this point on the grounds of the deposition of Admiral Nimitz.[113]

The evidence of the defense was extremely restricted. They worked with notes and papers which still happened to be in the possession of defendants or witnesses. Newspaper articles and press reports from earlier years were procured with difficulty. Getting books as evidence was also not easy due to the terrible destruction of German cities. The principal evidence was offered by witnesses. Their value was lessened, however, **[page 25]** since the supporters of the earlier times were themselves generally accused of war crimes and had a personal

---

[111] The Hague Conventions Respecting the Laws and Customs of War on Land of 1899 and 1907.

[112] Otto Kranzbühler was received at Nuremburg with a courtesy not extended to other defense lawyers. Since he was on active duty as a naval officer (working in the legal office of a German minesweeping unit which the British allowed to function to clear ports on the North and Baltic seas), he requested and was allowed to appear in court in uniform. Allied naval officers on the prosecution team treated him as an equal. He later defended German industrialists in subsequent war-crimes trials before developing a corporate law practice.

[113] Admiral Chester Nimitz, commander-in-chief of the US Pacific Fleet, stated it was general and approved practice not to attempt rescuing survivors of submarine attacks.

connection to the defendant as a fellow worker, secretary, adjutant or the like. It was of course impossible to bring to Nuremberg all necessary witnesses and those prepared to make a statement. Some had first to be laboriously tracked down in some camp. The Americans helped considerably in this, but in their grandiose and casual way. There were some funny mix-ups in the names which the Americans did not mind. Ribbentrop's defense was looking for Ambassador Dr. Fabricius from Bucharest as a witness. In his place a Ministerial Counsellor (*Ministerialrat*) Dr. Fabricius[114] from the Ministry of Economics sat in the witnesses' wing for months without knowing why and without ever being interrogated. A Criminal Counsellor (*Kriminalrat*) Dr. Geissler[115] was twice taken to Nuremberg, but it was a Dr. Geissler from the Ministry of Works who was sought as a witness for Sauckel. Two important witnesses for Sauckel were among those officials of the Reich who were not under suspicion or were only slightly incriminated. They were among those whom the Americans had collected soon after the occupation and had taken to Berlin for the purpose of administering common economic institutions (according to the Potsdam agreement). As this did not happen these people were forgotten. They were used occasionally for street cleaning and were down in the mouth and half-starved. At the last moment their whereabouts was discovered. They were brought by plane to Nuremberg and arrived there a few hours before their appearance in court. So besides their evidence, they had the opportunity by their appearance to serve as an example to the court of the American method of treatment. **[page 26]** Normally, however, they were careful of outward appearances. Witnesses half-starved in camps had

---

[114] *Ministerialrat* Dr. Paulus Fabricius confirmed this mix-up. He wrote to Ribbentrop's lawyer on 4 April 1946 that he had been mistaken for the former German ambassador in Bucharest, Dr. Wilhelm Fabricius, and that he, Paulus Fabricius, wished a discharge from "this place."

[115] *Kriminalrat* Dr. Kurt Geissler of the Reich Security Main Office was twice transferred to Nuremberg, supposedly as a witness for Sauckel. When he was finally interrogated he said that he did not know why he was there and knew nothing of Saukel.

the opportunity to eat great quantities before the trial and there were some nice dark suits which were loaned to those witnesses who looked too camp-like in their own things. Many a witness who was still free was not found, not wishing to be imprisoned. The Americans have, as I was told by a well-informed person, the custom at home to imprison witnesses, which is why after a car accident all the people run from the scene in order not to be arrested as witnesses of the incident.[116] From many witnesses, so-called affidavits were taken, statements under oath the authenticity of which had to be confirmed in writing by an American officer and which were then valid as evidence. The court had reserved the right to decide which witnesses would appear personally and which from whom only the affidavits were read out.

The Charter contained a regulation concerning the accused organizations, stating that each member of the organization could come before the court as a witness. When this became known in the camps a veritable flood of applications appeared. Signed applications were handed in by the tens of thousands. Working committees were formed in all the camps which prepared material for the defense. The court also named a lawyer for each organization. This unexpected onslaught could not be managed by one person alone. Preliminary elimination of witnesses was carried out in the camps by specially appointed persons. Over two hundred witnesses then came to Nuremberg. The majority of them were only allowed to hand in affidavits. For each organization about ten to twenty then appeared before a kind of preliminary court. **[page 27]** This was a second tribunal consisting of one representative for each signatory power as judge, plus lawyers for the prosecution and the defense. The hearings before this preliminary tribunal were intended to be recognized as fully valid evidence for the principal trial. Only some of the witnesses, I think four or six for each organization, then

[116] Rainer may have confused this with some type of protective detention as this comment is clearly not accurate. It is possibly based on erroneous hearsay.

appeared before the main tribunal.[117] Only the General Staff managed a really well-organized defense. Its most important representatives sat together for months in the Witnesses' Wing and systematically worked through material for the collective defense, which they discussed in detail with their lawyers at countless meetings. As the day of the hearing drew nearer, some important men from the English Prisoner of War camps, among them Field Marshall Rundstedt,[118] were also brought to Nuremberg.

The court saw to it that nothing could be uttered which might make any member of the victorious powers uncomfortable. The defense had to attach great importance to clearing up the early history of the war, especially dealing with the German-Russian treaty of August 1939 and its subsequent expansion with regard to the division of Poland. Ribbentrop[119] refused to mention the treaties in his defense, for, as I was told, he counted on Stalin repaying this loyalty by vetoing a death sentence. The case for the defense, however, needed these facts on record, having an eye on the hunger of the American press for sensationalism. The lawyer for Rudolf Hess[120] ventured to mention the treaties. He managed to raise a

---

[117] For the prosecution of Nazi organizations, the court ordered notices placed throughout Germany describing how concerned parties could apply to testify. Over 313,000 people responded, including affidavits from 155,000 people concerning the Political Leaders, 136,213 for the SS, 10,000 for the SA, 7000 for the SD, 3000 for the General Staff and OKW, and 2000 for the Gestapo. Six reports were compiled summarizing the contents of many of these affidavits. Defense Counsel also visited 80 internment camps and brought some 603 members of indicted groups to Nuremberg for screening as potential witnesses. The court then appointed a special commission under Lt. Colonel Airey M. S. Neave from Great Britain and five other commissioners, representing the four countries, to hear initial testimony. These commissioners heard from 101 applicants. Defense Counsel then requested that 31 of these witnesses be heard in court. In the end the Tribunal gave permission to hear the testimony from 22.

[118] Gerd von Rundstedt (1875-1953) was nicknamed "the high priest of strategy." Recalled from retirement he commanded armies in Poland, France, and Russia. His final posting was as commander-in-chief of the Western Front. After the war he served a brief imprisonment but was released because of illness in 1949.

[119] Joachim von Ribbentrop (1893-1946) became Foreign Minister in 1938 although he had no diplomatic or political experience. He retained his post until the collapse of the Reich.

[120] Rudolf Hess (1894-1987), Hitler loyalist and the party's deputy leader, had undertaken a mysterious flight to Scotland in May 1941, apparently hoping to end the war between Germany and Britain. In 1945, although declared sane to stand trial, his mental instability was evident.

goodly portion of them, until one of the Russians noticed what was happening and objected to the President, who then interrupted the lawyer, and reserved admission of the subject to a resolution of the court. **[page 28]** But it was enough for the American press to publish sensational reports the following day and this brought notoriety to the court. As a result the court allowed, to a limited extent, an interrogation of Ribbentrop's secretary and one from *Unterstaatssekretär* (Under Secretary) Gauss [sic][121] concerning this subject. It is significant for the development of international relations, that barely one year later it was officially announced by the American Department of State that all German secret documents on this matter would be made public.

The defense was greatly handicapped by the regulation of the Charter, that whatever was presented by the signatory powers had to be regarded as fully valid evidence. The Soviet prosecutor presented among others, a document of his government according to which Katyn[122] had been committed by the Germans. The General Staff was interested in destroying the credibility of this document and they succeeded by a roundabout way to have a line of argument concerning Katyn admitted. While in Nuremberg I got to know the witnesses who were later brought forward in this regard.[123] As I subsequently learned, the defense of the

---

Sentenced to life imprisonment he became the sole prisoner in Spandau prison from 1966 until his death in 1987.

[121] Friedrich Gaus, head of the Legal Department of the German Foreign Ministry in 1939, had drafted the Non-Aggression Pact (including the Secret Protocol) between Germany and USSR.

[122] In the spring of 1943 the Germans discovered mass graves near Katyn in the USSR containing the bodies of nearly 4400 men. The Germans determined that most were Polish officers shot by the Soviets. Stalin denied it and found support from his western allies for the notion that the Germans had committed the massacre. This point of view was not upheld at Nuremberg, resulting in the dismissal of Katyn as a prosecution charge. In 1952 Robert Jackson alleged Soviet responsibility for the war crime. Only in 1990 did the Soviets acknowledge their responsibility for the Katyn massacre.

[123] During his own imprisonment the Yugoslavs directed Rainer to comment on those Germans who might be informed about Katyn. He wrote a 158 page report in which he gave personality sketches on a number of Germans but he had little to say on Katyn. See Rainer's "Referete über verschiedene Personen in Verbindung mit dem russisch-deutschen Vertrage vom

General Staff succeeded, which meant that the Charter regulation concerning the conclusiveness of official documents was also devalued to a certain degree. After it was moved by the lawyer for Dr. Frick, the defense was also successful in quoting a witness to whom the prosecution had frequently referred without allowing him, for precautionary reasons, to appear before the court. This was Dr. Gisevius,[124] formerly serving in the Reich Security Main Office, and later emigrating to Switzerland. There he had exposed various stories concerning the *Reichstag* fire, the married life of Field Marshall Blomberg,[125] the death of Colonel General Fritsch[126] and the assassination attempt of 20 July 1944, which had been gleefully taken up by the world press and had been eaten up by the public. **[page 29]** At court it turned out that as an unimportant civil servant he had hardly been in the position to collect concrete material, and had simply passed on internal office gossip. Some of it proved to have contained notorious untruths. In one of the German newspapers edited by the Americans of Germany, I read a court report on the extremely poor impression people had of this witness.[127]

Jahre 1939," ARS-III, Inv 761, 80-4, II-46.

[124] Hans Bernd Gisevius (1904-1974) served in Switzerland as a German agent under cover as vice-consul. He came into contact with Allen Dulles, the US intelligence chief in Bern, who used him as a contact by those planning Hitler's July 1944 assassination attempt. After its failure Gisevius found refuge in Switzerland. His evidence before the IMT was, according to Judge Biddle, the most damaging testimony against Göring. In 1946 Gisevius wrote a controversial memoir, Bis zum bitteren Ende. Rainer's dislike of Gisevius reflected the opinion of Göring who called him "just a small-fry official."

[125] Werner von Blomberg (1878-1946), an exceptionally able staff officer, served Hitler as Minister of War and commander of Germany's armed forces. Forced to resign in 1938 because of allegations he had wed a former prostitute, he lived in obscurity until the end of the war. He died at Nuremberg while being held as a witness.

[126] Werner Freiherr von Fritsch (1880-1939), head of the Army High Command from 1934 to 1938, was a critic of Hitler's foreign policy. He was essentially dismissed in 1938 after a false accusation that he was a homosexual.

[127] Ingeborg Kalnoky, hostess at the Witness House where Gisevius stayed, observed that his personality was self-assured, self-important, and dogmatic. Göring was outraged that Frick's lawyer had called Gisevius as a witness, especially since he gave such damning testimony. Göring had to be forcibly removed from the courtroom.

But these few advantages gained by the defense could not make up for the over abundance of material the prosecution had from the beginning. It had been able to start working half a year earlier than the defense. Its work relied heavily on material which had been collected by a special commission[128] years before in the United States. One of the members of this commission was Dr. Kempner,[129] who formerly had been an official in the Ministry of the Interior and who had withdrawn in 1933 on account of his Jewish origin. He led the prosecution against Dr. Frick and there found an opportunity to take personal revenge. Hoards of experts in every field were available to the prosecution. While the spokesmen before the court were usually the same people, that is the chief and deputy prosecutors - with the exception of Dr. Kempner - the staff of experts alternated according to the field of work of each of the accused. For instance, after both Economics Ministers Funk[130] and Schacht[131] were finished, the numerous people sitting at the prosecution tables were replaced, except for the spokesmen. They then dealt with a new field, the Navy, with new experts, heaps of new files, and people familiar with the documents. After Raeder[132] this team disappeared **[page**

---

[128] Rainer is possibly referring to the special war crimes groups which were established in the late summer of 1944 to work with the Judge Advocate General's Department, US War Department.

[129] Robert M. W. Kempner, until 1933 a legal adviser to the Prussian Interior Ministry, had sought unsuccessfully to prosecute Hitler and the NSDAP on a charge of high treason. Dismissed and sent to a concentration camp, he eventually emigrated to the United States where he became a government attorney. In 1945, assigned to Jackson's staff, he served as head of the Defense Rebuttal Section. In 1951 he returned to a law practice in Frankfurt where he published widely on the Nazi abuse of power.

[130] Walther Funk (1890-1960), Hitler's Economic Minister from 1937 to 1945, received a life sentence at Nuremberg but was released in 1957.

[131] Hjalmar Schacht (1877-1970) was president of the Reichsbank and Economics Minister from 1934 to 1937. Raised in the United States he had pursued a career in German banking and played an important part in negotiating the Dawes Plan and the Young Plan. His role diminished after 1937 although he remained Minister without Portfolio until 1943. Cleared at Nuremberg he resumed his business career.

[132] Erich Raeder (1876-1960) was commander-in-chief of the German navy from 1928 until he resigned in 1943. He was succeeded by Karl Dönitz. Sentenced to life imprisonment he was released in 1955.

30] and a completely new set of people appeared for Schirach.[133] The staff attentively followed each phase of the trial and hearing, continuously thumbing their papers and passing on information to their spokesman. On the other hand the entire technical staff for the defense consisted only of the defense counsel, who had to be present throughout the whole trial and could only prepare his case in the evenings.[134]

The court room was on the third floor of the justice building.[135] It was about as long as the hall used for our Ljubljana trial,[136] but much wider, almost as wide as long. The court sat in the upper half of the long side and had the accused sitting directly opposite in front of the whole width of the room. The judges sat in a row side by side behind a raised covered table. Beginning at the right-hand side there were first the two Russians, then the two Britons arranged in such a way that Lord Judge Lawrence sat on the left towards the centre, then the two Americans arranged in such a way that Judge Biddle was next to Lawrence, then the two Frenchmen.[137] Behind each pair of judges was their national flag. The two

---

[133] Baldur von Schirach (1907-1974) was the Nazi Reich Youth Leader from 1933 to 1940. He was then appointed *Gauleiter* and governor of Vienna. Sentenced to 20 years imprisonment at Nuremberg he was released in 1966.

[134] This statement is not fully accurate since a number of the defense counsels had secretaries and assistants.

[135] Rainer's description of the court room which follows is accurate and conforms to that of other participants.

[136] The Syndicate Hall, Miklošičeva Street, Ljubljana, Slovenia.

[137] Each of the four powers appointed two judges, one regular and one alternate. All eight sat through the entire proceedings. The Russians were represented by Iona (or Iola) Timofeevich Nikitchenko and Alexander F. Volchkov. Nikitchenko was a major general of jurisprudence and vice president of the Supreme Court of the USSR; he died a few years after the trial. His alternate, Volchkov, a lieutenant colonel, was the Peoples Commissariat for Justice and professor of International Law in the Institute of Jurisprudence. The British were represented by Geoffrey Lawrence and Norman Birkett. Lawrence served as president of the court. His alternate, Birkett, was a judge of the King's Bench Division, High Court of Justice. He entered the House of Lords in 1947, dying in 1962 at age 79. The Americans were represented by Francis Biddle and John Parker. Biddle, the US Attorney General from 1941 to 1945, was originally from Pennsylvania. He later wrote his autobiography, In Brief Authority, and died in 1968 at age 82. Parker, born and raised in North Carolina, had been a US Circuit Court Judge since 1925. The French judges were

Russians wore uniforms, the six other judges wore civilian clothes and robes. All the judges were old. Lawrence is a small, stout man with an immense bald head. Biddle is tall with a high forehead. The second Englishman and the two Frenchmen looked like professors. The Russians did not give a military impression in spite of their uniforms.

The 21 defendants sat in two rows against the wall opposite the judges' bench. Behind them a row of American guards in white helmets with white belts and white gloves leaned against the wall. In the first row **[page 31]** from right to left were Göring, Hess, Ribbentrop, Keitel, Kaltenbrunner, Rosenberg,[138] Frick, Streicher,[139] Frank, Funk, Schacht. In the second row: Dönitz, Raeder, Schirach, Sauckel, Jodl,[140] Papen, Seyss-Inquart, Neurath,[141] Speer,[142] Fritsche [sic].[143] The soldiers wore uniforms without rank; the others wore civilian clothes. The defense lawyers sat at small tables in front of the defendants facing the judges' bench. A few long tables had been set up between the lawyers and the judges where stenographers for all four languages sat.

Henri Donnedieu de Vabres, a distinguished professor of law, and his alternate, Robert Falco, a veteran of both world wars and at the time of his appointment Chief of Counsel of the Paris Court of Appeal.

[138] Alfred Rosenberg (1893-1946) was a leading National Socialist philosopher who served as war minister in the occupied eastern territories. He was executed at Nuremberg.

[139] Julius Streicher (1885-1946), *Gauleiter* of Franconia, founded and edited the anti-Semitic paper Der Stürmer. In 1940 he was dismissed from his party positions for corruption and remained under house arrest for much of the war. He was executed at Nuremberg.

[140] Alfred Jodl (1890-1946) was chief of the operations staff of the Armed Forces High Command (OKW) from 1939 to 1945. Found guilty at Nuremberg, he was executed.

[141] Constantin von Neurath (1873-1956) served as foreign minister from 1932 to 1938. He then became Reich protector of Bohemia and Moravia until 1941. Sentenced to fifteen years at Nuremberg, he was released in 1954 for health reasons.

[142] Albert Speer (1905-1981) was Hitler's favorite architect. From 1942 to 1945 he was minister for armaments and war production. Sentenced to twenty years imprisonment, he became a best selling author on Hitler's Reich after his release in 1966.

[143] Hans Fritzsche (1900-1953) was head of radio broadcasting under Joseph Goebbels from 1942 until the end of the war. He was acquitted at Nuremberg but later convicted by a German denazification court in 1947. He was released from prison in 1950.

In the centre of the wider side, that is, to the right of the judges' bench at a diagonal was the witness box. This was a rather high platform, faced in wood, on which stood a small table and an armchair. The microphone was on the table. During his testimony the witness was seated, looked straight ahead down the length of the hall with the judges' bench on his left and the defendants on his right. The interpreters sat behind glass partitions to the right of the witnesses. They were clearly audible from the witness box and caused considerable disturbance. In front of the witness box there were the aforementioned long stenographers' tables, and next to them, facing the witness box, were placed a microphone and a tall lectern, used by the prosecutors and the defense lawyers. The judges' bench was therefore to the right and the defendants' seats to the left of this microphone. The witness on the one hand and the prosecutor (or the defense lawyer) on the other hand could look into each other's eyes during the testimony.

During the proceedings the defendants had permission and were able to write notes, passing them down to their lawyers or having a guard deliver them. They made continual use of this privilege.

Behind the microphone were the long tables for the prosecution placed end to end across the whole width of the hall. **[page 32]** As far as I could tell the English were at the extreme right, then the Americans, then the Russians and last the French. Behind them, across the whole width of the hall, was a wooden barrier; behind this several rows of seats had been constructed with room for about 50 journalists. Above this there was a balcony with rows of spectator seats for approximately 80 to 100 people. Admission tickets for spectators were handed out only after careful examination of personal information and for the most part only to foreigners. German spectators were bodily searched as attempted assassinations were feared. For most of the time the hall was almost empty, except when it was packed on the days with high profile testimony. The same thing was true of the press gallery.

The equipment for photography, filming and broadcasting was behind glass and was fixed to the upper parts of the walls. We were not aware of any of this activity which was nice. A modern artificial lighting system was installed. It shone through the glass cover and was just like natural light. This light was sufficient for taking photographs so that spotlights were unnecessary. The people in the pictures, however, had dark shadows from above, making them look rather somber.

The Americans took pride in their translation system.[144] The four languages used were English, French, Russian and German. The microphone carried each word which was spoken in one of these four trial languages from the judges' bench, the witness stand, or the lawyers' stand into the interpreters' cubicles; it was simultaneously translated by the interpreters into the three other languages. The translated word was then transmitted through the interpreters' microphones. **[page 33]** The interpreters did this simultaneously and independently. On each seat for the judges, the defendants, the lawyers, the witness, the representatives for the prosecution, the press and the spectators there were earpieces which could be taken off a rack and used. There was a device on the earpieces for tuning in to the desired language. If the declaration before the court was in your chosen language you heard it directly, that is to say as it was being spoken. Otherwise you would not hear it through the microphone, but after a short pause you heard the translated text. Thus each person present could follow the trial in his own language. Because the earpieces did not fit tightly you could usually hear the words spoken in the hall with your other ear, and then if you were tuned in to another language you would also hear the translation. In the witness box you heard in addition the babble of voices from the interpreters' cubicles in

[144] The Nuremberg process was the first occasion simultaneous translations were used on such an extensive basis. The League of Nations had employed translators to work from one language to another, but the IMT was the first where four different languages were used. IBM, which had been working on a simultaneous translation system, provided the equipment while a native Frenchman, Leon Dostert, from Georgetown University, and Eisenhower's personal translator, played a prominent part in developing the technique.

your other ear; initially in this hubbub it was not easy to distinguish which was the actual text. Because of this system it was necessary to speak slowly and in short sentences. Even the stenographers often made imploring signs for people to speak more slowly. If a person spoke too quickly the President or one of the interpreters could switch on an amber light which lit up in front of the speaker and signified that he must speak more slowly. If the President wanted to interrupt a speaker he switched on a red light, whereby the whole sound system immediately became inoperable. As an example, the President used this means when the defense counsel mentioned the Poland Treaty and the Russian objected. Everything spoken **[page 34]** was recorded on disks.[145]

The entire system worked rather well which the Americans always mentioned with pride in the newspaper. There were, however, also break-downs. Once a whole day's proceedings were lost because of a break-down. When it was my second turn as a witness on 13 June 1946, Lawrence had barely opened the proceedings when some of the listeners signaled that one language, I think it was English, was not coming through. Lawrence recessed, but the court remained in the hall. After about fifteen minutes the Marshall announced that the system was in working order again, and Lawrence continued, but after a few minutes there was another break-down. Now the court withdrew to their room and the trial was interrupted for almost an hour, during which the Americans, with red faces and in a state of great anxiety, attempted to repair it. In such instances they always thought right away of German sabotage or used this as an excuse.[146]

A Court-Marshall with the rank of captain was in charge of the technical aspects of the trial. He asked the people present to take their seats when the proceedings were about to begin. Then he announced that the court was about to enter and instructed everyone to stand. The court always entered in a solemn

---

[145] The US Army Signal Corps recorded the trial on disks, magnetic tape, and write recorders while court reporters compiled a transcript.

[146] The system of simultaneous translations was new, subject to break downs, and as the IMT staff acknowledged, "complicated."

procession in single file through a special door right beside the judges' bench. Everyone else including the defendants were already in the hall. Upon recess the court marched out just as solemnly. The witnesses waited in the Marshall's room prior to their testimony until they were called and would enter by a special door next to the witness box. The wait in the Marshall's Room was memorable for each witness and much talked about because the American guards in there, **[page 35]** being genuine Americans, were slouched in their chairs with their feet up on the tables. There was even a guard in the chair in front of the Marshall's desk with his feet on it. When the Marshall, who was after all in a captain's uniform, entered the room none of them moved, and if he needed something from the desk drawer he first pushed the guard's feet aside so that he could get into it. Most of the time the guards were asleep or reading comics, which are colored booklets with adventure series in pictures, the primary educational material of American soldiers. I thought the descriptions by previous witnesses to be slightly exaggerated, but then I was amazed by what I saw with my own eyes. These, however, were not the only American customs which astonished us as German soldiers.[147]

The court was in session on week days from Monday to Friday. The session began at 10 o'clock in the morning and lasted to 1 o'clock with a break of 15 minutes. Then followed an hour for lunch. The defendants remained in the Palace of Justice where they were given their lunch. Of course they were allowed to talk to each other. The afternoon session lasted from two to five o' clock with a fifteen minute break. At Christmas and before the summaries began there were longer recesses of one to two weeks. The defendants always had to be present except in the case of illness. Kaltenbrunner was absent for some months having suffered an injury of the brain caused by grave mistreatment while in English

---

[147] Rainer took great pride in his military service as a regular soldier in Norway for several months in 1940. He later held the rank of lieutenant in the reserves. The informality of the American soldiers contrasted sharply with the strict formality with which Rainer was familiar.

captivity.[148] He was in hospital and during the trial was close to death on two occasions. On application some of the defendants were permitted to be absent with their lawyer a few days before their court appearance in order to prepare their testimony. **[page 36]** Most of the defendants followed the whole of the long trial very attentively, especially Göring. Only Hess read a book most of the time which he had open in front of him, and often stayed away. He enjoyed special consideration owing to his state of mind.

Defendants or witnesses were transferred to the American army hospital only if their life was considered to be in imminent danger. Field Marshall Blomberg, although having retired in 1938 and having had nothing to do with the war, was nevertheless imprisoned in the witness wing. At his advanced age he suffered from serious dropsy.[149] He could no longer walk, was taken care of by younger officers and was taken to hospital only eight days before his death. *Reichsschatzmeister* (Reich Treasurer) Schwarz in his late seventies was confined to bed in his cell in the witness' wing with serious heart problems and was tended by Eigruber[150] and me. As this could not continue he was taken to Herzbruck Camp to hospital. During my six month stay in the witness' wing there were only three people who received hospital treatment. They were Field Marshall Blomberg who died, an old admiral with serious diabetes and an old State Secretary with a fractured femur, both of whom recovered.

---

[148] Rainer may have gleaned this view from Otto Skorzeny who claimed that Kaltenbrunner was locked in the Tower of London and tortured daily, although Peter Black, Kaltenbrunner's biographer, reports that there was no hard evidence of physical mistreatment. The ten weeks of confinement and intense interrogation in London, however, produced major psychological strain so that Kaltenbruner arrived at Nuremberg a broken man. Sitting in his cell he would suddenly start crying, prompting one of his guards to comment that he was the biggest "crybaby" in the prison. Headaches and cranial hemorrhaging occasionally kept Kaltenbrunner from the court room.

[149] A disease in which watery fluid collects in the cavities or tissues of the body.

[150] August Eigruber (1907-1947) held a number of positions in the Austrian Nazi party before the *Anschluss*. From 1938 to 1945 he was *Gauleiter* of Upper Danube. In 1947 he was tried and executed by the Americans.

For the prosecution the American Jackson played first fiddle. He was a Supreme Court judge in Washington, a close confidant of Roosevelt, the principal initiator of the war crimes trials, the president of the International Commission for the Verification of War Crimes,[151] ambitious, hot tempered and a hateful enemy of Germany. He took over the cross examination of the most important defendants himself, although he came off a loser with Göring. **[page 37]** An American newspaper reported: One to nothing for Göring! His first deputy was an American colonel who advocated a moderate tone for which he was dropped at Christmas 1945.[152] His second deputy was Dodd,[153] known as the most handsome man of the court, a dark, slightly Semitic type, middle aged, very elegant, and snappily dressed, with a marked vanity and conceit in his bearing. He was patterned after his boss. The British prosecutors were Sir Shawcross[154] and Sir David Maxwell-Fyfe.[155] Sir David is a well-known member of the Labor Party, was very caustic, yet had the reputation for advocating justice. Among the French I only remember Alphonse de Menthon,[156] a well-known professor of law who

---

[151] Again Rainer meant the United Nations War Crimes Commission.

[152] Rainer is confused on this issue. Colonel Robert Storey, Jackson's deputy as Executive Trial Counsel, did leave the prosecution in mid-January 1946, but his departure was according to a pre-trial arrangement with Jackson.

[153] Thomas J. Dodd had prosecuted espionage, sabotage and war fraud cases during the war as Special Assistant to the US Attorney General. After Nuremberg he served his home state of Connecticut in Congress, first in the House, then the Senate. He died in 1971.

[154] Hartley Shawcross had had a distinguished war record in civil administration. In the general election of 1945 he entered Parliament where he was immediately chosen Attorney General in Clement Attlee's Labor Government. Later he became a successful corporate lawyer. Although he was the chief British prosecutor, he delegated day-to-day tasks to David Maxwell-Fyfe.

[155] David Maxwell-Fyfe, member of Parliament since 1935, served during the war first as Solicitor General, then Attorney General under Winston Churchill. He conducted the negotiations which led to the Four Power Agreement under which the International Military Tribunal was established. He was later elevated to the peerage as Earl Kilmuir.

[156] Francois de Menthon left Nuremberg immediately after his opening address in January 1946 to accept a political appointment in Paris. He was replaced by Auguste Champetier de Ribes who had led the resistance movement "Combat" during the war.

answered the general objections of the German International Law Professor and Defense Lawyer (*Deutsche Völkerrechtsprofessors und Verteidigers*) Dr. Jareiss [sic][157] with substantive arguments. The principal prosecutor for the Russians was Brigadier General Rudenko.[158] His first deputy, a general or a colonel, according to a newspaper report, shot himself while cleaning his pistol.[159] As it was unusual for such a high ranking officer to be cleaning his own pistol, the rumor arose that he had been accused of having consorted too much with the Western Allies and had committed suicide. Since then the Russians apparently were said to have avoided all social contact with the Western representatives.

The greatest sensation was caused by the scandal concerning Jackson, which broke out on 12 June 1946, the day of my first court appearance. Jackson had hoped to become Chief Justice of the Supreme Court at Washington as a reward for his zealous attention to duty. Truman, however, nominated the Secretary of the Treasury Fred Vinson to the post as he had to be rewarded. This made Jackson furious and while in Nuremberg he distributed a statement to the American journalists which appeared in the press on 12 June 1946. **[page 38]** Here he declared that he was passed over as a result of machinations by his old enemies in the Supreme Court, and particularly Judge Brown[160] who had plotted against him. Then he went on to say that Brown had previously had a lawyer's office which was now being run by his former partner, and that he continued to

---

[157] Hermann Otto Emil Jahrreiss, born in Dresden in 1894, was a law professor who later worked editing the IMT papers.

[158] Roman A. Rudenko later became the Procurator General of the Soviet Union, the highest legal position in that country. He was also the chief Soviet prosecutor in the trial of the American U-2 pilot, Gary Powers, who was shot down over the Soviet Union in 1960.

[159] According to Rudenko, General N. D. Zorya, the prosecutor who had introduced Field Marshall Paulus' testimony, accidentally shot himself while cleaning his gun. Jackson's investigators reported, however, that it was highly unlikely a Russian general would be cleaning his own gun, particularly with the barrel pointed between his eyes. Drexel Sprecher, an assistant trial counsel and prosecutor in all thirteen Nuremberg trials, maintained that his suicide came after the disclosure of the secret protocol to the German-Soviet Non-Aggression Pact of August 1939.

[160] Rainer meant Justice Hugo Black.

receive a share of the profits. As a judge he procured cases for this office and then favored them. The ensuing article in the press caused a huge sensation and resulted in a scandal never before seen in the history of American justice. Brown replied in a factual manner and stated that the attacks were unjustified.[161] It was evident that Jackson's wounded pride drove him to this. Americans are known to have a huge respect for justice and Jackson suffered the worst possible reproach over there among the puritan Americans, that is, of having violated this image. Even months later I found articles and cartoons in American magazines about this scandal, all pointing to the same basic notion: it had always been known that the judges of the Supreme Court quarreled, but never had anyone dared to wash their dirty laundry in public. In June Jackson was called to America, returned briefly to Nuremberg for the summaries and the verdicts, and was then relieved of his duties.[162] His successor was Major General [sic] Taylor[163] who was said to be of the same school.

The reports in the American press were to a certain degree unbiased, as far as I could tell. They reported all the essentials of the trial and fished for sensationalism. Their tone was that of a sports journalist describing a football match between a home and a foreign team. **[page 39]** Though it is obvious in each line that he wishes his own team to win he also lists the goals and highlights of the opponent's play, thus glorifying the victory of his own side. The German press took great pains to emphasize that it did not want to have anything to do

---

[161] Jackson, the upright Yankee, and Black, citizen of the deep South had constant clashes. Nonetheless, Jackson's attack created a sensation, especially since it brought a feud in the US Supreme Court into the open. Jackson's letter to the Judiciary Committee of the Senate was unprecedented. Some in Washington called for both to resign while others feared the public controversy would damage the prestige of the IMT.

[162] Jackson was not relieved of his duties. Once the main trial was over Jackson returned to the Supreme Court where he served until his death in 1954.

[163] Telford Taylor had held numerous U. S. government legal positions. When Jackson asked him to help at Nuremberg, however, Taylor had no special interest or experience in international law. From 1946 to 1949 he served as the chief prosecutor in the subsequent Nazi trials, i.e., in this sense he was Jackson's successor. He held the rank of Brigadier General.

with the past twelve years. It regarded the allegations of the prosecution as proven and the declarations of the defense as mere pretext. Only one particular reporter from the Süddeutsche Zeitung[164] struck me by every now and then broaching general problems and thus hinting at his being worried as to the effects of the trial on future international relations. As to the broadcast reports I could only listen to them during the three weeks I spent in Langwasser Camp. Every evening at eight fifteen a commentator spoke about the trial.[165] He was a well known Austrian Jew from Radio Vienna with a French sounding name which now alludes me.[166] You could not reproach him for being unbiased. He gave a distorted view of the events. The effect of his utterances was put into question by a regular 2 p.m. program in which excerpts from actual recordings from the trial were played. There I could listen to parts of the defense summaries, impressive - to me at least - by their calm representation of the facts and their adherence to a legal objectivity. In Dachau I heard that parts of the defendants' closing words were also transmitted in this way and made an impression.

At the beginning of the session the President read out a declaration from the American President Truman: **[page 40]** the American government had agreed that the Russian prosecutor also bring evidence of events in the territories of the Baltic states Estonia, Latvia and Lithuania. This, however, was not seen on the part of the United States of North [sic] America as a recognition of the annexation of these states into the USSR.[167]

---

[164] The Süddeutsche Zeitung, published in Munich with a circulation of 410,000, was one of 21 newspapers licensed by the Americans.

[165] German radio stations in Nuremberg and Munich broadcast a 15 minute nightly commentary on the trial. In addition, the Armed Forces Network (AFN) transmitted news of the trial to over 50 outlets. Although meant primarily for US soldiers, many Germans listened to AFN.

[166] Probably Gaston Oulman, appointed by the military government. Countess Kolnoky, who served as hostess of the Witness House, commented that Oulman had a decided dislike of Germans.

[167] The indictment of the major war criminals made reference to Soviet claims of sovereignty over the territories of Estonia, Latvia, and Lithuania. The United States government,

The trial (began if I am not mistaken on 10 December 1945 - I set the record straight according to information available to me: it) began on 20 November 1945, with the presentation of materials and arguments by the prosecution.[168] The four prosecutors counsel had divided the material among themselves according to factual and territorial categories, presenting it in the following order: American, English, French and Russian. On 7 March 1946, the defense of the accused individuals began, according to the order in which they were seated. First came the appearance of the defendant, presentation of the defense material, followed by the testimony of the defense witnesses. Later on - about the end of June, the beginning of July 1946 - the defense lawyers gave their summaries for the individual defendants. Then it was the turn of the six organizations, and it was again: presentation and argumentation by the prosecution, presentation and argumentation by the defense, summaries by the defense. Then followed the summaries of the four principal prosecutors and the closing statements of the twenty-one individual defendants. This lasted until about mid-September 1946. Then a break of about two weeks followed. On 30 September 1946, the court pronounced the guilty verdicts and the judgments with regard to the three acquittals. Each of those found guilty then had the opportunity to make a comment about the degree of punishment. On 1 October 1946, the defendants were called forward, not collectively as previously, but one after the other, and heard a short pronouncement regarding their sentence. The sentences were subject to final confirmation **[page 41]** by the Interallied Control Council.[169] The petitions for pardon were also sent to this body. The sentencing was

---

in a letter of 6 October 1945 from its chief prosecutor, Robert Jackson, raised reservations about these claims but did not wish to delay the proceedings by insisting upon a change of wording. At the same time the United States insisted that its acceptance of the indictment should not be construed as recognizing such sovereignty.

[168] This strange sentence construction may result from Rainer's corrections on the original which were not properly corrected by the typist.

[169] The Allied Control Council.

confirmed in every case. The petitions for pardon were rejected. The executions took place on 16 October 1946 beginning at midnight. Those sentenced to imprisonment were sent to Berlin-Spandau according to newspaper reports.[170]

The Nuremberg trial was conducted according to the usual principles for criminal trials in England and America. The Anglo-Saxon criminal trial differs considerably in part from those in Germany and most continental European countries.[171] Interestingly enough, it has developed from the old German criminal trial as has been codified in the *Sachsenspiegel*.[172] While German law in Central Europe was significantly modified by the acceptance of Roman law, in England the old principles were retained and came from there to America. Here in Europe, it is the presiding judge who has the main responsibility for conducting the trial. He is the spokesman, interrogates the defendants and examines the witnesses. The prosecutor and the defense lawyer are given the floor. They may make a motion and with the presiding judge's approval they are allowed to ask the defendants or the witnesses supplementary questions. Here, it is the presiding judge's duty to bring out everything that may be useful in finding out the truth in an unbiased way. The assessment of evidence depends entirely upon his judiciary discretion. It is his duty also to consider all aspects that might exonerate the defendants. In case of questionable evidence the following principle is

---

[170] Dönitz, Funk, Hess, Neurath, Raeder, Schirach, and Speer went to Spandau on 17 July 1947, some nine months after sentencing. The delay was due to prison renovations.

[171] Drexel Sprecher, who was Assistant Trial Counsel at Nuremberg, explained the difference in a 1998 interview; his comments parallel those of Rainer: "You see, there's a difference between continental law, and the Anglo-Saxon law. In . . . [continental] law, the prosecutors tend to pour in their materials. The judge looks it all over. And then the judge takes the leadership in questioning and so forth. That's quite different than in the Anglo-Saxon process, where the judge knows practically nothing before the trial starts. And it's up to the prosecution to do all the leadership in presenting the evidence."
(Interview with Nuremberg Trial Prosecutor Drexel Sprecher, Court TV Law Center, 1998, www.courttv.com/casefiles/nuremberg/sprecher.html)

[172] The *Sachsenspiegel* (Saxon Mirror), the most important of the medieval compilations of Germanic customary law, was collected in the early thirteenth century and written in the vernacular. It showed little Roman influence, largely because it had not encountered Roman law.

applicable: *in dubio pro reo.*[173] In the Nuremberg trial this did not apply. The prosecutor and the defense lawyer dominated the proceedings. It was not the presiding judge who interrogated the defendants and the witnesses. The prosecutor called the witnesses for the prosecution to court **[page 42]** and asked them his questions. They answered him. When the prosecutor had finished, the defense lawyers were allowed to question the witness for the prosecution, that is, to cross-examine him. This latter procedure is the main feature of the Anglo-Saxon trial. It was the same when the defense lawyer called his client to the witness-box and questioned him and later on the respective witnesses for the defense. It was the prosecutor who had to carry out the cross-examination. The whole thing is simply a dialog between the prosecution and the defense during which each side arrives with an army of witnesses and written evidence. This is exactly like the 7, 14 or 21 oath helpers of the *Sachsenspiegel.*[174] The responsibility of the presiding judge is merely to oversee the order of the court. He would give the floor to the prosecutor or the defense lawyer and would allow him to proceed. If a question or an answer was not relevant to the trial he would rap a pencil on the table, demanding that he speak to the point. He swore in the witnesses and also the defendants who were interrogated as witnesses (!) for their own cases. During their interrogation as witnesses they were not addressed as defendants but as "witnesses." It only happened extremely rarely, but it caused a sensation each time when Lawrence or Biddle asked a witness a supplementary question. The other judges kept absolute silence.

The evidence could not be assessed in an independent manner, but only within the confines of a rigid system. The court must accept as proven everything presented by one side, if there is no objection by the other. Thus, fighting the assertions of the other side is the main task of those involved in the trial. Only an

[173] "When in doubt favor the defense."

[174] With the *Sachsenspiegel*, an accused, in court, was required to prove his assertions by swearing a solemn oath to the truthfulness of his declarations. He had, however, to be supported by oath-helpers who testified to his truthfulness. Custom generally specified the number of oath-

assertion that has been challenged needs to be proven. The burden of proof rests with the one who brings forward the assertion. Evidence is presented by documents and witnesses.

With **[page 43]** documents, it is important that they are recognized as pieces of evidence and entered into the court record as such. On this point the prosecution at Nuremberg had an enormous advantage. Based on the aforementioned clause of the Charter, all official documents of the signatory powers were fully valid pieces of evidence. Therefore they were automatically entered into the court record. When the prosecution presented documents, the defense objected in most cases and the court had then to decide whether the document would be entered into the court record or not. If a document was accepted the only avenue open to the opposing side was to destroy its credibility and thus take away its reliability as conclusive proof.

In the case of the witnesses, the court at a closed meeting decided who would be admitted. Then it was crucial to get as much information as possible from the witness and to incorporate it into the trial records. The question-answer game between witnesses and the lawyer for each side was therefore prepared in advance. The witness had been informed beforehand which questions his own side would ask and had already prepared his answers. In most cases he had discussed it with the appropriate lawyer, who, if he was a defense lawyer, had also discussed it with the defendant. Therefore, dangerous questions or questions, which if answered, would have compromised the oath, were usually, if not always, discarded beforehand.

During questioning the opposing side could object to the admission of a particular question. Then the presiding judge gave a ruling. During cross examination, one's own lawyer could object to questions of the other side, if by answering, the witness would possibly **[page 44]** incriminate himself. In such cases the presiding judge could forbid or allow the question, or he could leave the

---

helpers required.

decision up to the witness whether he wished to answer. During cross examination it is a popular method to ask for an answer of yes or no, and then to put the question in a way that the answer is unfavorable in any case. Then the opposing side or the witness himself can appeal to the presiding judge for permission to answer the question more fully.

When a witness is cross-examined by the opposing side after having been questioned by his own lawyer, it is not so important to refute single details, but rather to undermine the credibility of the witness and make him appear in a bad light. The idea was to make the witness nervous and confused, entangle him in contradictions, and make him lose control and be led to speak notorious untruths. For this, drastic measures were used. A great number of defense witnesses, including myself, had already been questioned ahead of time by the prosecution, and only afterwards did we come in contact with a defense lawyer. During cross examination the prosecutor tried to point to contradictions by comparing prior statements with current evidence. Apparent contradictions arose quite frequently, because the questions asked on these two occasions were quite different. Added to this there were many mistakes and contextual misrepresentations made by poor interpreters, and minutes of the interrogations were not read to the witness.[175] The prosecutor liked to isolate single sentences from their context which often gave a completely different meaning. It was necessary to keep control of oneself to avoid being confused by such attacks.

The most popular method of the prosecution when trying to discredit a defense witness **[page 45]** was to describe him as a war criminal and, without warning, accuse him of his own war crimes that did not have any connection with the trial but did succeed in affecting the witness. This happened to the field marshals Kesselring and Milch,[176] to *Gauleiter* Bohle[177] and others. It was

---

[175] Rainer is referring to his own interrogations at Nuremberg, the minutes of which he never saw.

[176] Erhard Milch (1892-1972) played a key role in running the *Luftwaffe* during the war. Imprisoned as a war criminal, he was released in 1954, after which he worked as an industrial

extremely drastic in the case of *Gauleiter* Lauterbacher,[178] who earlier had been Chief of Staff of the Hitler Youth. He was supposed to give evidence for Schirach. In the witness box, he had barely said his name when the American prosecutor interrupted the defense lawyer and shouting, questioned the witness whether he knew that he indeed had had 50 Poles poisoned. Lauterbacher denied this immediately, but Schirach's lawyer was so shocked that instead of protesting against this kind of question and the interruption, he abandoned most of the questions and tried to remove the "dangerous" witness from the court room as quickly as possible. Later on I read in a newspaper that because of this affair Lauterbacher was tried before an English military court at Minden and was found not guilty, as not a single word of this was true.[179] As I have been told, this practice leads to quite grotesque behavior on the part of both sides in the United States, because most of the time truth is not important, but only the success of the moment. The presiding judge usually intervenes only if he is asked to do so by the opposing side.

If you compare the whole Anglo-Saxon trial with a game of soccer, which is very similar, the umpire only whistles in a case of foul if the opposing side explicitly claims the foul. Otherwise his intervention is restricted to gross violation of the rules; it is his main duty to keep the game going. This also was the case **[page 46]** at Nuremberg. The presiding judge only objected to questions

---

consultant in Düsseldorf.

[177] Ernst Wilhelm Bohle (1903-1960) was head of the *Auslands-Organization* (A.O.), the group which dealt with the affairs of Germans not living within the borders of the Reich. Imprisoned for a brief time after the war he subsequently became a businessman in Hamburg.

[178] Hartmann Lauterbacher (1909-1988) was Baldur von Schirach's chief of staff in the Hitler Youth from 1933 to 1940. He then served as *Gauleiter* of Southern Hannover-Brunswick until 1945. Interned after the war he escaped in 1947, eventually returning to Germany where he died at Seebruck/Chiemsee in 1988.

[179] Rainer is confused on this point. Lauterbacher gave his testimony for Schirach on 27 May 1946. Upon cross-examination Thomas Dodd examined him closely on the issue of ordering 400 to 500 prisoners poisoned or shot. There was an intense exchange, but it was part of the cross-examination.

and answers if they were too long winded or wandered too far from the topic. In such cases the speaker could quickly explain why he had digressed and he was often allowed to continue.

For the German side this method of trial was new and unfamiliar. Even though they had made themselves familiar with this unaccustomed form of procedural law in theory, the German defense lawyers lacked experience, whereas the Americans were masters at it. They [the Germans] completely failed during cross-examination in putting biting questions to the prosecution witnesses, who were questioned first, and in undermining their credibility as the Americans did later on in the case of the defense witnesses. They thought they could refute the arguments of the prosecution by their own factual arguments. I remember how bewildered the German defense was when first Göring himself was interrogated and then the witnesses for his defense with whom Justice Jackson performed a true American cross-examination. Whereas Göring was a match for his opponents and could not be intimidated, some of his witnesses came off poorly. It was a mistake not to examine the prosecution witnesses rigorously and the German defense were not able to recover. Most of the German defense lawyers were dignified elderly gentlemen who never got used to the foreign methods during the entire trial and most certainly had inhibitions owing to their own legal traditions. Only a few younger gentlemen adapted quickly, especially the naval defense lawyer, Dr. Kranzbühler, who was perhaps the only one able to fight on equal terms. **[page 47]** In the course of the entire trial two completely different legal systems were diametrically opposed to one another, and the weaker party, that is, the German side, was disadvantaged.

I experienced this in a very real way during my own cross-examination as witness on June 13, 1946, when the presiding judge introduced a procedural debate. He announced that on the basis of a motion from the prosecutor, the court had decided that the time for the defense lawyers' summary would be restricted to a total of 14 trial days. The first person to contradict this was Keitel's lawyer, Dr.

Nölte [sic],[180] a dignified old gentleman. He spoke directly to the point and made it clear that the prosecutor had not ordered any restriction, that there had been no discussion about this with the defense and that time would be too short for a regular defense. Lawrence answered that there had been talks about it with individual Germans. Then the lawyer for Neurath[181] spoke, who in the meantime had calculated how much net time there would be if the intervals for translating were taken into account, and stressed very impressively that because of its serious nature and the world wide interest, this trial ought not to be exposed to the accusation that the defense did not have adequate opportunity to do its duty. Then Prosecutor Dodd answered that this was usual in America and that this was also valid for Nuremberg. Dr. Kubuschek [sic],[182] Papen's lawyer, replied and proved on the basis of examples from international legal practice that until then there had been no restrictions for the defense in any international trial. The law that was to be applied here was not American but international procedural law. Then the Russian prosecutor, a colonel spoke and began by saying **[page 48]** that in the Soviet Union neither the prosecutor nor the defense counsel were restricted regarding their freedom of speech. After these words there was some tension as to whether the Russian would take a stand against Dodd. But after a short interval the Russian concluded that he would support Dodd's proposal. While everyone in the audience looked at each other in bewilderment because it did not seem to make sense, Lawrence, thinking there had been a mistake in the translation, after having spoken quietly with Biddle for a few minutes, closed the debate by saying that the court would think over the defense arguments and make a final decision.

---

[180] Rainer meant Dr. Otto Nelte, a veteran of the First World War and a member of the Nazi party from 1933 (except for the period 1935 to 1938 when his membership had been declared invalid).

[181] Otto Freiherr von Lüdinghausen, born in Berlin in 1881, studied law in Leipzig. He was never a member of the Nazi party.

[182] Egon Kubuschok, born in Upper Silesia, studied in Breslau, and practiced criminal law. During the war he defended the head of the Czech resistance movement before the People's Court in Dresden.

As I heard later, the allowed time for speaking was prolonged, but it still remained restricted.[183] From this debate I got the impression that Lawrence conducted the trial firmly and that he tried in an objective way to keep a balance between the prosecution and the defense. Otherwise - as far as I, a German lawyer, may comment - the behavior of the German defense impressed me as being more objective and representative of a more solid legal tradition.

All the trials in the American zone against concentration camp personnel and concerning the murder or mistreatment of airmen are held at Dachau. There, a custom has developed according to which American and German lawyers share the defense. I was a witness for the prosecution in a trial at a superior American military court and had to give evidence about Adolf Hitler's methods of issuing orders to the Party.[184] I had the opportunity to observe the abrupt and rapid verbal duel between the two Americans, which started after every second or third question. As a result, **[page 49]** the presiding judge always decided whether the question was to be allowed at all, and if so, if it was formally correct. The presiding judge made his decision quickly and the cross-examination was hardly ever delayed. It was only then that I saw how a real American criminal trial usually works and how interesting and gripping its course can be when both sides are equal and well-practiced. I also heard that generally the American defense lawyers at Dachau made an honest effort, and saw it as a matter of good sportsmanship to represent their clients well. It was also the practice for the Americans to alternate as prosecutors and as defense lawyers on different occasions, so that, as an American explained to me, they had a feel for both sides and would not become biased.

---

[183] Otto Stanmer, as spokesman for the defense, asked for one day per defendant. Lawrence agreed. He did not wish to give the defendants any reason to attack the fairness of the trial.

[184] Rainer was a prosecution witness in the trial of former *Kreisleiter* Emil Breitenstein, 18 to 20 September 1946 in Dachau. Breitenstein, whom Rainer did not know, was accused of shooting an American POW.

Once, during the trial of another *Gauleiter* concerning the murder of a pilot, I had a lengthy discussion with an American defense lawyer, who was Jewish, and a German defense lawyer. I was astonished at the fairness and the zeal the American showed in the case of his client. During the Eupen-Malmedy trial[185] which was conducted against members of the *Leibstandarte* [186] who allegedly had killed prisoners, the American defense lawyer went as far as appealing directly to Truman and the Congress in Washington, in order to obtain a revision of a judgment he considered unjust. During the trial against guards of the Flossenburg [sic] concentration camp the American-German defense enjoyed complete freedom of movement and were able to present such comprehensive evidence that the verdict was even accepted by the German side as being severe but just.[187] In both trials the American defense lawyer unearthed **[page 50]** the fact that during the pre-trial the CIC had extorted incriminating statements from the defendants by torture, which was common in Oberursel.[188]

---

[185] The process involving 74 members of the *Waffen SS* accused of murdering 81 American POWs near Malmedy which began at Dachau on 2 May 1946. Although 43 death sentences were handed down none was ever carried out; subsequent reviews and the desire to win German support during the Cold War led to reductions in the sentences.

[186] The *Leibstandarte-SS "Adolf Hitler"* was the unit primarily responsible for Hitler's personal safety. Eventually attached to the *Waffen-SS*, it grew to division size and gained a reputation as an elite fighting corps.

[187] The Flossenbürg trial, 12 June 1946 to 22 January 1947, concerned 46 guards charged with killing, beating, and mistreating prisoners. The trial, before an American Military Tribunal at Dachau, found all but 5 of the defendants guilty. Fifteen were executed and the remainder received prison terms ranging from one year to the eleven who received life imprisonment.

[188] Although Albert Speer called Oberursel "the notorious interrogation camp" where there was rough treatment, screams, and anxious replies, an unrelated event sheds different light on Rainer's accusation. The US military intelligence investigated reports of American mistreatment of German POWs in September 1945. The authorities interrogated 171 inmates, asking each prisoner two main questions: first, whether he personally had been mistreated, or had witnessed mistreatment of others; and second, if he gave a positive answer, was he prepared to make a sworn statement. Only nine made sworn statements. One of these, the Austrian, Herman Neubacher, generally gave second hand accounts of alleged mistreatment. Most prisoners stated that their treatment was "at least satisfactory and beyond criticism," although there were general statements about the loss of personal possessions.

The prosecutors at Nuremberg were not only well-versed in procedural tricks, they seem also to have used methods in Europe that have to be described as unusual. I have just explained how, while I was giving evidence, a point of procedural clarification was deflected. It was a regular occurrence for quotations from earlier speeches, writings or statements to be taken out of context and re-introduced in an incomplete and absurd manner. Often witnesses angrily claimed that additions had been made by someone else. During the court session, Kaltenbrunner accused Justice Jackson of having forged signatures and minutes. I was unable to check whether these complaints were true and therefore I relay them with this reservation.[189]

When comparing the two methods of trial, under normal circumstances I should like to favor the Central European process. An impartial presiding judge, who directs the interrogations himself and sticks to the principles of every civilized jurisdiction, who also considers exonerating facts, can arrive at the truth in a totally different way than the umpire of the American trial. The danger of errors of judgment is lessened if the pre-trial, too, is conducted by an investigating judge, as specified for the Austrian criminal trial. This objective is even more pertinent in cases where the defense (with the right of motion and appeal which is obligatory in cases of imprisonment) is brought in during the course of the pre-trial. **[page 51]** Unrestricted assessment of evidence on behalf of the court is a definite advantage and an improvement compared to the rigid requirement to prove the case as in the Anglo-Saxon trial, which is reminiscent of the medieval *Sachsenspiegel*. The dueling role that both lawyers have to play can mar the proceedings. I have already mentioned instances like this. The fact that the prosecutor is forced into the same pattern of behavior as the defense lawyer

[189] Kaltenbrunner's disagreements were not with Jackson but with Colonel John Amen. When Kaltenbrunner testified in his own defense Amen presented him with a letter bearing his signature; Kaltenbrunner said it was not his. He also denied receiving summary reports which had his name on them.

undermines the dignity which is expected of them as representatives of the public interest.

If the continental European trial process is to be valued more highly it is imperative that the court is completely objective and allows itself to be guided only by the search for justice while seeking the truth. If the presiding judge is determined from the outset to favor the prosecution and conducts the trial only from the point of view of the prosecution, and in so doing, intentionally neglects developments favorable to the defendant while completely restricting the defendant's ability to defend himself before and during the trial, or if the defense attorney is reduced to a mere semblance of a legal representative, this trial is without any judicial and moral value. The American procedure must be preferred to such a trial, because at least it puts both sides on an equal footing. It may be that the American trial has survived precisely because of the unregulated circumstances in the Wild West where there were neither impartial legal standards nor impartial judges. There the only possible legal decision consisted of guaranteeing "fair play" to the contending parties.

In an international context, it seems to me that things are similar wherever **[page 52]** neither impartial legal standards nor a body of impartial judges are present. With the American trial a real defense *must* exist at least in a rudimentary form, because otherwise the whole "game" would not take place. The whole process trial is based so much on the polarity between the prosecution and the defense, that if one side were absent the other side would lose its function. In the case of the other type of trial the defense lawyer only needs to sit there like an extra, yet the formal method of procedure for a trial is well preserved. With the American trial, the defense counsel *must do* something, otherwise, to retain the image I portrayed, this is no longer a soccer *game*, but rather a team training session without an opposing side present. In spite of this it is possible to secure the desired political slant as the London Charter showed in theory and the Nuremberg Trial showed in practice. At Nuremberg, one team was exceptionally well trained, excellently equipped, familiar with the field and knew the referee favored them. The other team had never played together before, were not trained, wore street shoes and unsuitable clothing, were not used to the field and the rules of the game, and knew the referee and the public were against them. Yet they were allowed to come on to the field, play defensively, and even score some goals. The referee conducted the game fairly, observing all the rules. In the case of any disadvantage on the part of one side, there is still the tendency to prefer this process when dealing with a subjectively defined area of law as in political trials.

I shall refer to some other occurrences during the course of the trial. Göring sat for about a week in the witness box **[page 53]** and had occasion to speak about the events since the takeover of power. He spoke openly, while mindful of his responsibility, and came off very well, as we saw from the reaction of the Americans with whom we were in contact. He told much that was news to me and explained circumstances I had not understood up to then about events in the Reich concurrent with the takeover of power in Austria. It was an interesting statement of his that Himmler and Heydrich had ordered the killing of the Jews on their own without informing the *Führer*.[190] That might explain why the *Führer* never mentioned a word about it to us *Gauleiter* and *Reichsleiter*. Göring requested that his lawyer visit him frequently and then chatted with him about all kinds of things except the trial. His lawyer, Dr. Stahmer,[191] had not known him earlier, but was captivated by his personality. Göring was generally acknowledged to be the outstanding personality among the defendants. It has remained a mystery how he succeeded in obtaining the poison with which he

[190] Göring testified that he did not know about the Jews, nor did Hitler. He said, "My opinion [is] that the Führer did not know about details in concentration camps, about atrocities as described here. . . . This is also explained by the fact that Himmler kept all these matters very secret." (TMWC, vol. IX, 611, 614.)

[191] Otto Stahmer, born in Hamburg in 1879, had practiced law since 1907. During the war he had worked on civil and labor cases from his home in Kiel.

killed himself immediately before the execution. As a consequence of this event, the prison commander, Colonel Andrus, lost his job.[192]

Hess refused to enter the witness box and did not wish any defense at all. He only agreed that evidence could be given in the case when it was made clear to him that the corps of Political Leaders would be exonerated by it. He himself, however, did not take part. In the summary he spoke just as he had before 1941. When the defendants were allowed visits by their wives he refused to see his.[193]

More than the other defendants Kaltenbrunner behaved in accordance with the characteristics of the American judicial procedure and put up a fight **[page 54]** with Justice Jackson, enthusiastically reported by the American newspapers.[194]

Rosenberg had prepared extensive quotations from his works for the proceedings in order to refute once and for all international misinterpretations. But not everything was admitted as evidence. Thus nine tenths of his real activity remained beyond the scope of the trial. As an American officer told me, for the purposes of the court, only what Rauschning,[195] Otto Strasser[196] and Konrad

---

[192] Although Andrus may have been criticized because of Göring's suicide, he was not dismissed. When he did return to the United States in early 1947 the War Department issued a statement stating that his departure was in no way connected to the suicide.

[193] Hess had not seen his wife and son since 1941. Even later in Spandau prison he refused to see them. Not until he was in hospital in 1969 did he request to see his family. The first visit lasted 30 minutes.

[194] Kaltenbrunner put up a spirited defense, which surprised many people including one or two judges. He occasionally embarrassed the prosecution on cross-examination.

[195] Hermann Rauschning (1887-1982), born in West Prussia, was appointed President of the Danzig Senate in 1933 after a Nazi election victory. He fled to Switzerland in 1935, renouncing his political convictions, and wrote books warning of the dangers of Nazism. At the end of the war he was living in the United States.

[196] Otto Strasser (1897-1974) was a leading Nazi politician in the North German wing of the NSDAP (along with his brother Gregor). After differences with Hitler he resigned from the party in 1930. During the Nazi period he lived in exile but returned to Germany after the war where he was active in right wing politics.

Haiden [sic][197] had written about the intellectual substance of National Socialism was relevant.

Frank had written a diary consisting of twenty volumes[198] on his activities and his thoughts at the time which had fallen into enemy hands. The prosecution used quotations from it.

With Funk an extraordinary case of indiscretion occurred. A letter he had written to his wife after the verdict was published by the army newspaper "Stars and Stripes" together with derisive remarks.[199]

Schacht pretended not to belong to the group and in the witness box he took pains to show off his well-known sarcastic wit.[200]

The justification for the verdict in Dönitz's case is remarkable. He was found guilty only on two counts: 1. that he used submarines offensively and thus took part in the war of aggression, and 2. that he had not annulled the order[201] when taking over the Navy and thus had violated the customs and practices of war. In this connection it is necessary to know: re 1) at the beginning of the war Dönitz was *Kapitän zur See* (colonel) and had about twenty boats at his disposal. re 2) that the order had been issued by the *Führer* **[page 55]** and was passed to the units via the officers commanding the three components of the *Wehrmacht* just as

---

[197] Konrad Heiden, one of the National Socialist's earliest opponents in 1923, wrote a critical account of Hitler in 1944: Der Fuehrer: Hitler's Rise to Power; his book was re-issued in 1969. Heiden called himself "one of the oldest anti-Nazis now in the United States."

[198] The Nuremberg trial records indicate that the diary consisted of 38 volumes.

[199] "Funk Denies All Charges in Letter to Wife," Stars and Stripes, 25 September 1946. The letter was written after the verdict.

[200] Telford Taylor later wrote of Schacht, "[He] could be charming, but he did not suffer fools gladly and was arrogant, tough, sarcastic, and domineering. . . . For most of his colleagues in the dock he had no use, and they, understandably, found him most unlikable." (Telford Taylor, The Anatomy of the Nuremberg Trial – A Personal Memoir (New York: Alfred A. Knopf, 1992), 383.)

[201] This reference is to the "Commando Order" issued by Keitel at Hitler's insistence on 18 October 1942, which instructed that captured commandos, whether in uniform or not, should be killed rather than taken prisoner. Dönitz passed the order along to the navy.

hundreds of other orders during the war. This order said: enemy sabotage units caught disguised in contradiction to the Hague Convention were to be shot. According to the German point of view the order to shoot is based on the Hague Convention. But, however this may be, these two counts of guilt seemed so extraordinary to a military mind that the wish to dispose of the last leader of the German Reich must be regarded as the real motive.[202]

When Raeder was called to Nuremberg the rumor went around that he was a Russian prisoner of war and had already begun to take part in building up a large fleet. This was said to be the real reason why he was lined up with the principal war criminals. I learned from a notice in an English newspaper that the British had concerns in this regard. According to the article Admiral Saalwächter[203] and another German admiral, whose name I have forgotten, gave lectures at the Marine Academy in Leningrad. In his petition for pardon Raeder asked that the sentence of life imprisonment be changed to death by firing squad.[204]

When the two admirals were on the stand a strong delegation from the Royal Navy was in the spectator's gallery. An English admiral is said to have commented: if the Nuremberg principals were generally applied there would be no admiral in the world who would not have to be sentenced in exactly the same way.

---

[202] Eugene Davidson, The Trial of the Germans (New York: Collier Books, 1966) argues that the charges against Dönitz, especially the orders concerning treatment of shipwrecked crews were no different from what the Allies practiced. What damned him was his pro-Nazism, blind devotion to the *Führer*, anti-Semitism, and the fact that he was Hitler's successor.

[203] Alfred Saalwächter (1883-1945), born in eastern Prussia, was involved in the conquest of Norway and then became commander of the Baltic Station. Captured by the Soviets he died in their custody.

[204] The Control Council rejected the request. Among other reasons Article 29 of the Charter forbade the Council to increase punishments; it could only reduce them.

Influenced by a statement of Commandant Hösch [sic][205] of the Auschwitz Concentration Camp, Schirach declared Adolf Hitler a murderer and anti-Semitism a crime. **[page 56]** The American psychologist Gilbert[206] –a Jew– ran enthusiastically about in the witness wing with the hand written declaration and wanted to start a big propaganda campaign. One witness told him that there was no more anti-Semitism in Germany anyway. Gilbert answered that he believed that too, but that the growth of anti-Semitism in the United States was becoming quite dangerous and something would have to be done about it. In this connection may I mention a story that happened to *Gauleiter* Bohle and which he told me immediately afterwards. Bohle speaks English fluently. An American soldier came up to him asking if Streicher had actually been the one who had had the Jews killed. Bohle answered evasively that in fact this must have been Himmler. The American replied that it did not matter whether it was Himmler or Streicher, but they would need one of the two in America in order to settle the Jewish problem.

Papen declared at the beginning of his evidence that he was the representative of the "other Germany." Soon after his acquittal, an English newspaper wrote, it had become clear that the people who were ministers today in Germany were no good. Government should be transferred to the only two capable people, Papen and Schacht.

In the case of Fritsche [sic], who was in charge of the German radio news service throughout the war, the establishment of guilt is remarkable. He had

---

[205] Rudolf Höss (1900-1947) fought in the First World War, receiving the Iron Cross. He served 5 years in prison for a violent murder, joined the SS in 1934, and was eventually posted to Dachau, Sachsenhausen, and then Auschwitz (1940) where he was Commandant. He was executed by Polish authorities in 1947.

[206] Gustav (Gus) Gilbert, who was Jewish and a member of CIC, spoke fluent German and had trained as a psychologist. At first he served as Douglas Kelly's translator but when Colonel Andrus asked him to act also as an "observer" of the Nuremberg prisoners he became a prison psychologist. He later testified at Adolf Eichmann's trial and had a distinguished career, including 17 years as Chair of the Department of Psychology at Long Island University. He died in 1977 at age 65.

never incited hatred and he never consciously presented untruths.[207] Official reports of the *Oberkommando der Wehrmacht* [High Command of the Armed Forces or OKW] had been behind certain announcements which did not accurately represent the facts.

Seyss-Inquart's counsel, the Viennese lawyer Dr. Steinbauer,[208] **[page 57]** presented abundant evidence that leading personalities of the Christian Social and the Social Democratic parties in Austria had made positive comments regarding the *Anschluss* both before and after the event. He quoted the unanimous resolution of Vienna's Provisional National Assembly of 12 November 1918, stating that German Austria was part of the German republic. He also quoted the unanimous reiteration of this resolution by the constituent members of the National Assembly who were elected on the basis of universal suffrage in the Statute of the Republic of German-Austria adopted on 12 March 1919. A press interview that the current Federal President Dr. Karl Renner[209] had given after the *Anschluss* caught the attention of the public. In this interview he welcomed the *Anschluss* as the fulfillment of a dream desired by all Germans.[210] Furthermore, in a letter written to Hitler by Federal Chancellor Dr. Schuschnigg from the concentration camp where he lived in a house with his family and a servant-girl (!), he declares himself to be in favor of the accomplished *Anschluss*, objecting

---

[207] Fritzsche, a very minor figure compared to the other defendants, was generally seen as a stand-in for Paul Josef Goebbels, the propaganda minister; he was also one of only two defendants captured by the Russians. Even Göring acknowledged his minor role. Upon meeting Fritzsche after his acquittal, Göring said, "Very glad you've been acquitted. We had a bit of bad conscience as far as you are concerned."

[208] Gustav Steinbauer, born in Vienna in 1889, had practiced law since 1921. Although the Gestapo declared him unworthy to be an army officer he served in the German army as a sergeant from 1944 to 1945.

[209] Karl Renner (1870-1950), a Social Democrat politician and jurist, was Austrian chancellor from 1918 to 1920. From 1931 to 1934 he was president of the National Council, but withdrew from politics after the victory of Austro-fascism. From 1945 to his death he was the president of the Second Austrian Republic.

[210] See Renner's interview, "Ich stimme mit Ja" ["I vote with yes"], Neuen Wiener Tagblatt, 3 April 1938, 3.

only to the treatment of the Catholic Church.[211] Also Dr. Steinbauer quoted a declaration which the former Senator of Idaho, William G. Borah had given in 1938 and which said: "The Anschluss of Austria was natural and inevitable and did not touch America's interests." Prosecutor Dodd objected to this being taken into the record and the court reserved decision on the matter.[212]

I quote the following passages from the closing statements of the defendants which were kept short, as they appeared in the Neue Zeitung[213] [sic re no italics] of 2 September 1946, issue nr. 70: **[page 58]** Rosenberg: "...in Germany I have demanded freedom of conscience in accordance with my philosophical convictions and I have made a similar concession to each of my opponents and have never been party to any religious persecution." He described the National Socialist view as "the noblest concept which had been wrestled with for more than a hundred years and for which a symbolic banner was raised."[214] Frick: "...the whole of my life has been given to serving my people and my fatherland. To them I have dedicated my best energies doing my duty with the utmost loyalty. I am convinced that no patriotic American or citizen of any other country would have acted differently, for any deviance from this manner of behavior would have

[211] During Schuschnigg's confinement at Sachsenhausen, December 1941 to February 1945, he lived in a small residence and had a maid to assist the household. Although it is doubtful he ever approved the *Anschluss*, he may have favored the German acquisition of the Sudetenland.

[212] The Stars and Stripes (19 May 1946) quoted Steinbauer reading Borah's 1948 statement: "The Anschluss with Austria was natural and inevitable and none of America's business.'" Steinbauer's quotation does NOT appear in the published transcript of the trial proceedings.

[213] The Neue Zeitung, with a circulation of 1,200,000, was a semi-weekly newspaper published by the US in its zone.

[214] Rainer's statement differs slightly from the translation in the Trial of the Major War Criminals before the International Military Tribunal (TMWC): "In Germany, in pursuance of my ideological convictions, I demanded freedom of conscience, granted it to every opponent, and never instituted a persecution of religion." Concerning National Socialism, Rosenberg said, "I understood my struggle, just as the struggle of many thousands of my comrades, to be one conducted for the noblest idea, an idea which had been fought for under flying banners for over a hundred years." (TMWC (Nuremberg: International Military Tribunal, 1946-1949), XXII, 382-383.)

been a breach of my oath of allegiance, namely high treason."[215] Seyss-Inquart: "To my mind Adolf Hitler will always remain the man who will go down in history as the creator of Greater Germany. I have served this man. What came then? I can not today shout 'Crucify him' having shouted 'Hosanna' yesterday."[216]

As to the executions the American press published extensive reports, even giving details of the technical procedures. The hangman,[217] an American sergeant, gave interviews. The family magazine "Life" published large photographs of the hanged men. You see each of them lying on a board, a thick rope next to him. Keitel's and Frick's faces are full of blood. The caption says that the blood was not caused by a prolonged and torturous death, but that it was quite usual for blood to come forth from nose and ears. The official report said that death was established after so many minutes; for each of them the time was about fifteen minutes. Later a statement was added that there had been rumors **[page 59]** that the death agony had lasted that long. That was not true. Death ensued immediately, but was confirmed by the doctors only after about fifteen minutes. Reading the first declaration and at the same time looking at the photos in "Life" a person is left wondering.[218] Göring's suicide was discussed extensively. I read an

[215] Rainer's account again differs slightly from the Nuremberg records: "My entire life was spent in the service of my people and my fatherland. To them I have devoted the best of my strength in the loyal fulfillment of my duty. I am convinced that no patriotic American or citizen of any other country would have acted differently in my place, if his country had been in the same position. For to have acted any differently would have been a breach of my oath of allegiance, and high treason." (TMWC, XXII, 385.)

[216] The Nuremberg record records Seyss-Inquart's final statement as: "To me he remains the man who made Greater Germany a fact in German history. I served this man. And now? I cannot today cry 'Crucify him,' since yesterday I cried 'Hosanna.'" (TMWC, XXII, 405.)

[217] Master Sergeant John Wood, the hangman from the US Third Army, claimed to have "dropped" 347 men in his fifteen year career prior to Nuremberg. He later died in an accident while engaged in the Korean War.

[218] Roy Martin, one of the three doctors in attendance at the executions, noted in his book: "As an army physician officially participating in, and observing the executions, it is my opinion that the victims were properly hung. . . .No one ever said hanging was neat. . . . [But] not one body had any injury to his nose, nor were there bodies with blood spattered on their faces and shirts, except for Frick, who scraped his scalp as he swayed, just as he fell through the trap door, and scraped the side of his head." Martin further commented that with hanging loss of

especially detailed description in "Stars and Stripes" of Streicher's last moments. He entered the execution chamber calling out "Heil Hitler," then shouted several times "Purimfest 1946"[219] and at the end said to the Americans: "The Bolsheviks will hang you just like this one day." The rest of them uttered short and dignified last words, but Rosenberg said nothing. According to the newspaper report all the equipment used for the executions was burned to prevent the establishment of any cult, and the ashes of the executed men were scattered from an airplane.[220] In spite of the fact that the prison commander had strictly forbidden it, Father Sixtus dedicated the next mass to the salvation of those executed.

At first the three acquitted men were not able to leave the Palace of Justice because the German police were waiting for them in front of the doors, having been ordered by the Denazification Commission to arrest them again. They gave interviews to the American journalists, for which Schacht demanded chocolate. Later all appeared before tribunals, Schacht in Stuttgart, Papen and Fritsche [sic] in Nuremberg. I have no information as to how it ended for them.[221]

[Editor's note: Rainer's Postscript, which consisted of three pages, fits best at this point and has been moved.]

---

consciousness was instantaneous, but that it took between 8 and 17 minutes for the heart to cease. Only then could death be pronounced. (Roy Martin, Inside Nurnberg: Military Justice for Nazi War Criminals (Shippensburg, Pennsylvania: White Mane Books, 2000), 70, 96-97.)

[219] Purim, a Jewish holiday, celebrates the deliverance of the Jews from massacre by Haman, chief minister to King Ahasuerus (commonly identified with Xerxes). Haman had persuaded the king that Jews were useless and should be eliminated. But Esther, the king's Jewish wife, interceded and as a result it was not the Jews but Haman who perished. The story is recorded in the Book of Esther.

[220] Although there is no official version of what happened, J. Persico, Nuremberg: Infamy on Trial, asserts that following cremation at Munich's East Cemetery, the ashes were emptied into a small stream, the Contwentzbach, which subsequently emptied into the Isar River. Drexel Sprecher, in his extensive account of the trial, says that the corpses were taken to Dachau where they were cremated and the ashes emptied into the Isar River.

[221] Fritzsche was found guilty of war crimes by a German court and served three years. He died in 1953 at age 53. Schacht, sentenced to eight years by a German court, was cleared on appeal in 1950. He began a new career in finance, specializing in the Third World, and died in 1970 at age 93. Papen received an eight year sentence from a German court in 1947, but was released in 1949. He died in 1969.

[page 77] Postscript. I am going to add some events I have remembered only while writing this.

The Russian prosecution unexpectedly presented two witnesses which caused a sensation. One was Field Marshall Paulus.[222] He gave evidence of the orders he had been given for the battle for Stalingrad. He wore civilian clothes and looked good. In the corridor of the building a German woman asked him how the German prisoners in the Soviet Union were treated. He answered: "Good." The second witness was a Russian metropolitan who was giving evidence about the destruction of churches by the Germans. The newspapers wrote that he had a long beard, wore a priestly robe and had a big golden cross hanging on his chest.[223]

Of the six accused organizations three were acquitted; they were the government of the Reich, the General Staff and the SA. The following were declared to be criminal organizations: the corps of the political leaders, the SS, the Gestapo with the SD. The group of people in this category was clearly defined and restricted. The court established that in each case personal guilt would have to be proved by individual trial.

The Soviet judges objected to the acquittals of the three individual defendants and the three organizations as well as to some - not all - non-capital sentences, and published a statement which did not concur with the justification for sentencing.[224]

---

[222] Friedrich Paulus (1890-1957) was the commander of the Sixth Army in the assault on Stalingrad. After surrendering to the Russians he assisted them by appealing to German troops on the eastern front to desert. Released from Russian captivity in 1953, he took up residence in East Germany until his death.

[223] This was the very Reverend Nikolai Ivanovich Lomakin, Archdean of the churches in Leningrad, who gave his testimony on 27 February 1947.

[224] Nikitchenko issued a ten thousand word dissenting opinion in which he opposed the acquittals of Fritzsche, Papen, and especially Schacht; the refusal to find the Reich Cabinet and the General Staff and High Command criminal organizations; and the unwillingness to sentence Hess to death.

There ensued a quarrel between the Russians and the Americans concerning the press reporting at the executions which is why the Russians stayed away from the event.[225]

[page 78] This was the end of full consensus for the remaining international war crimes trials. The whole of the Russian delegation departed. The French suggested all the members of the three organizations found guilty be put before international courts, divided into several groups, and punished. This did not happen. In Nuremberg only the Americans remained, led by Major General [sic] Taylor as the new principal prosecutor. The further Nuremberg trials - against medical doctors, against Field Marshall Milch, etc. - are being run by an exclusively American military court. Similarly, in other zones and countries, trials are taking place before national courts.[226] This main trial might well remain the only one before an international military tribunal of the four signatory powers, the subject of this treatise.

In Dachau the Americans have devised a new method for dealing with the many thousands of low ranking personnel in the concentration camps. They formed committees of previous prisoners before whom the defendants had to appear on a brightly lit stage, the so-called stage show or Revue. The prisoners then "recognize" the guards and say what they are guilty of. The American defense had concerns and once, unknown to the prisoners' committee, succeeded in having a number of American soldiers dressed up in camp uniforms sent to the

---

[225] Rainer mistook the British opposition for the Russians. The Allied Control Commission had responsibility for the executions. To the discomfort of the British, the Council accepted the American suggestion that representatives of the press be present, a necessary precaution against rumors and legends. The British judges objected to the decision. Each of the four countries represented on the ACC sent two representatives as witnesses. There were also eight journalists, including one each from Pravda and Tass. One of the three doctors in attendance was a Russian.

[226] Thousands of Nazis were tried before allied military tribunals in the British, French, Soviet, and US zones. In addition, Nazi war crimes trials were held in other countries including Denmark, Poland, Czechoslovakia, and Yugoslavia. In 1946 the International Military Tribunal for the Far East charged 28 Japanese war criminals with war crimes. Later, officials of both the Federal Republic of Germany and the German Democratic Republic prosecuted over 25,000 former Nazis.

stage show. The prisoners "recognized" most of them and stated the cruelties they had committed. Since then they have become more cautious, but the stage show has remained. The convicted next come in groups of eight **[page 79]** before a lower American military court with three presiding judges and are sentenced by summary jurisdiction. There are prison sentences between two and five years, but also acquittals or referrals to a Higher Military Court which has authority to impose the death sentence.

The millions of petty and minor war criminals - according to news reports over two million in Bavaria alone (the Süddeutsche Zeitung [sic] reports that opposing them characteristically were 15,000 people who described themselves as "victims of the system" from the 12 years of Nazi rule) - in the occupied zones of Germany and Austria are being subjected to various procedures collectively known as "denazification."[227] The proceedings are described at the same time as a criminal trial, as atonement, as reparation, as a process of administration, as a means for cleansing, as penance, as a special contribution to the process of rebuilding or whatever; they are sometimes written, sometimes oral; there is or is not the right of appeal; sometimes there is a hearing of evidence, often there is not; sometimes counsel for the defense is admitted, usually not. The consequences for the defendant are: imprisonment up to ten years, forced labor, loss of property, loss of position and acquired legal claims, a ban from working in his trade or profession, fines, special taxes, loss of home, surrender of furniture and clothing, special work without payment, loss of franchise, loss of freedom of association, of an academic degree, etc. But also through general decrees by mayors or special deputies measures were imposed on people who were merely

---

[227] Denazification aimed at removing the discredited Nazis and replacing them with a new ruling elite; it had questionable results. Although it was fairly radical in the Soviet zone, in the West it became a case of cumbersome bureaucracy, relative inefficiency, selective opportunism, and unintended consequences. It suffered from a lack of clear direction: was the aim to cleanse Germany of Nazis or cleanse Nazis of the stain of Nazism? Eventually the Germans themselves inherited denazification from their conquerors, but the process soon disappeared as a result of the Cold War.

members of the party or associations and against whom no action can be taken. Such measures are loss of dwelling, (page 80) surrender of furniture and clothing, unpaid extra work removing rubble, procuring firewood, cleaning streets, etc., special fines, and contributions for public purposes, etc. The unsystematic, uncontrolled, and subjective application of all these measures in random fashion has led to a general feeling of legal insecurity much discussed in the press. What will be the final outcome is hard to say, probably the same as with the big war crime trials: much unhappiness and a negative impact on the future.

[Editor's note: return to page 59 and the conclusion of Rainer's manuscript.]

The question could still be asked whether the initiators of the trial fulfilled their objectives. In so far as they sought to eliminate the top functionaries of the Third Reich by means of a legal process they have succeeded. This approach could be characterized as a non-traditional continuation of war by one side. **[page 60]** The propaganda effect is indisputable. For months, and if one includes the rest of the trials of war criminals, for years the international press was furnished with material which is intended to keep that mood alive as was done both before and during the war. There were always complaints in the press concerning the passive attitude of the German population towards the Nuremberg trial. Explanation for this attitude was given in this way: the German people are still stunned by the defeat, and they are concerning themselves only with the problems of everyday life and do not wish to see or hear anything more about the war. It was announced that the material of the prosecution was going to be published and would be obtainable in book form. Since there was no talk of publicizing the materials of the defense, prominence could be given to one-sided propaganda.

I doubt whether the trial will one day be seen as a true resolution of the matter of war guilt. In world history it has always been that observers of the time assign guilt to the vanquished and never to the victors. But this does not settle the question. The German documents were certainly used freely, but not in a form that can stand up to scientific scrutiny. The prosecution published and quoted according to their own needs, but not according to the internationally accepted methods of scholarly research. The international scholarly community investigating the question of war guilt will not be pleased with the material presented in court and will probably have to start all over again. It seems doubtful whether the material will still be available then and whether it will be possible to re-establish it in its original form. (page 61) The historian views nothing of greater significance than interpreting historical sources according to the political or legal context of their times. Then the irreparable flaw will come to light that only the German material, and not the material of the opposing side was used. This may seem in order for the criminal trial, but in order to shed light on the question of war guilt, investigating the process of political development stage by stage by comparing the documents of both sides is essential. Who knows if any of the victorious states will decide to publish their secret material at all or at some point in time. Historical research in every country cannot do without this material and therefore will press for it. As experience has taught us this happens sooner or later, often after a change of government; then, and only then the objective and scientifically definitive research into the causes of the war begins. Then the national researchers pursue it and begin to work with colleagues in other countries. After the First World War things also happened in this way. After ten years there was a totally different picture than the one declared at Versailles in 1919. The question also arises as to why the victorious powers did not publish their material at the time of the trial. With their good conscience that would have provided resounding support for their position!? The German people are highly interested in getting an objective and a clear picture in regard to the causes of war. The assertions from Nuremberg do not appear to do this and are too reminiscent of the declarations of the previous regime during the war which were just as one sided. When Stalin, in a speech in 1946, sees the main cause of both world wars as being the unjust distribution of goods on earth and from that leads on to alluding to the imperialistic expansionary tendencies of Germans, Italians, and Japanese, he comes closer to the truth than all the assertions of the Nuremberg trial.[228] **[page 62]** Such a realistic perspective, in which there is no shortage of harsh comments against the defeated power, furthers much more the peaceful revision of the untenable state of affairs and with it the maintenance of world peace than does the whole gigantic infrastructure which Mr. Jackson set up in Nuremberg.[229]

There is still the open question whether future wars can be prevented, impeded, or humanized as a result of the Nuremberg trial and the remaining trials of war criminals. I am quite sure this will not be the case and I maintain that the opposite will happen. If by chance there were idealists among the victors who believed in this, they will in a future time declare the war crime trials a catastrophe for all the peoples involved. On this point, international criticism began before the Nuremberg trials were over. A victor may never judge the defeated in a trial, for he is then prejudiced as a judge. He is given the role of judge, not by an impartially binding provision of law nor by an internationally valid treaty, but rather by virtue of the victory of his weapons. What rights his victory actually allow are expressed in the conditions of the peace treaty. They may be of the utmost severity, if the good sense of the victor and the general situation permit. But never does military victory entitle anyone to make himself judge with regard to the preceding war to which the victor was just as much party as the defeated, both having fought for their own national interests. No clause of international law valid up to now **[page 63]** is based on the provision that the victorious state is made judge over the defeated one. This clause will never be

---

[228] On 9 February 1946 Stalin spoke to a group of voters in Moscow. Among other points he blamed both world wars on the development of capitalism and its uneven development.

[229] Rainer shows here the opportunistic nature of his personality. While a prisoner of the English 8th Army he had spoken and written as a proponent of the British position. Now, as a Yugoslav prisoner he projects a position more favorable to the Communist East.

contained in any future international treaty, for it will never be voluntarily signed by any state on earth. Thus the London Statute[230] and the proceedings based on it will never be an item in a prior agreement for peace and establishment of rights. This is only possible after a war and can be repeated in the same form only after a future war. Every nation must therefore conclude from this, that if they were to lose a future war their statesmen, politicians and generals will suffer the same fate as the Germans do now. Each nation will therefore fight with everything they have, for only military victory can spare them from a similar fate. There will be no statesman and no general who will advise ceasing operations, who capitulates in order to avoid further sacrifice, for they will remember the fate of the German statesmen and generals. There might still be traitors who hand over intelligence to the enemy for the promise of impunity. Reich Commissioner Seyss-Inquart faced such a dilemma in the Netherlands when confronted by the demands of Eisenhower's chief-of-staff Lieutenant-General Bedell-Smith.[231] The American reported this incident in an article in "Life" magazine. From this point on, after Nuremberg, all future wars will be fought to the bitter end, without restriction and without consideration for the rules of war, until the complete and utter destruction of all possible resistance. This condition will last until such time as new international treaties solemnly ban the principle: the victor is the judge, **[page 64]** or until there is only one world victor who, as Rome since Augustus or as Mongolia under Genghis Khan, views every war as a revolt against world order and with his God-given right to be world ruler punishes those waging war as

[230] The London Charter.

[231] Walter Bedell-Smith (1895-1961) was a staff officer who rose through the ranks, becoming Secretary of the US Joint Chiefs of Staff. In September 1942 he went to England where he became Chief of Staff to Eisenhower, remaining with him to war's end. He established the basis for negotiation of the Italian armistice in 1943 and arranged the surrender of German forces in the West in May 1945.

Seyss-Inquart met Bedell-Smith on 30 April 1945 where one point of their discussion concerned the flooding of the land for military defense purposes. Bedell-Smith accepted that the flooding to that date was militarily justifiable, but "'if you flood any more now, it is no longer justifiable.'" Seyss-Inquart, who had carefully defied a scorched earth policy as ordered from Bormann, testified that after 30 April there was no more flooding.

rebels. There is no doubt that the Americans are quite preoccupied with thoughts of this kind, but they do not correspond to international law up to now and sharply contradict the principle of national sovereignty.

The Geneva League of Nations was built on the principle of equal rights for free and sovereign nations. All members were equal. There was no resolution by which one country would have submitted its sovereignty to the majority in the General Assembly. As on the occasion of the Briand-Kellog [sic] Pact[232] the question of sanctions was discussed but failed because of the opposition of the Great Powers who did not allow any minimization of their sovereignty. The Hague Court is based on the same principles. It does not provide extradition or punishment of single persons. Only neutral states are allowed to participate as members of the Court in cases of controversy.

The United Nations is based on different principles. If a comparison is made between the League of Nations and a democracy of nations, the UN appears as an aristocracy. The five victorious supreme powers: the USA, Great Britain, the USSR, France and China are predominant. They are permanent members of the Security Council and, protected by the right of veto, cannot be outvoted. They form the supreme command and are to provide the contingents for a kind of world police. **[page 65]** A supreme court should be shaped according to similar principles. Roosevelt conceived the collaboration of the five great powers such that each gives up a part of its sovereignty and is in accord in general questions with the four other powers while being protected in crucial matters by the right of veto. His hidden agenda was probably to form, that is to say, buy with dollars, a safe majority for the USA of the votes of the medium sized and small states, and thus in effect play a leading role in the UN; in so doing the US would become

---

[232] The Kellogg-Briand Pact, also called the Pact of Paris, condemned the use of war to solve international problems and called for the peaceful settlement of disputes. By 1934 some 64 nations had signed it. But it had a major weakness since it provided no method of enforcement. Although there have been numerous violations, the pact has never been rescinded or replaced. It served as part of the legal basis for Nuremberg.

dominant in the world. If this plan had succeeded one could imagine a further development of the system of justice established at Nuremberg, leading to the formation of a clear world supremacy by the USA. Rather than succeeding, this plan failed. Thus the Nuremberg example lost all significance as a basis for a legal system. The union of the five aristocracies fell apart immediately following the Potsdam conference which rather than leading to future collaboration, gave rise to a hostile mistrust. Since Churchill's Fulton speech on 6 March 1946,[233] it has become universally clear that the world has been split into two blocks, each of which is firmly resolved not to sacrifice one grain of its sovereign rights in favor of common interests.

The USA is still behaving as if it were prepared to make concessions in favor of the UN, but this attitude will only continue as long as there is an assurance of a majority of votes. No American Congress would hand over the atomic bomb to an international organization, if there were the slightest danger of the USA being outvoted. The Soviet Union is acting in the same way. The two most important problems for maintaining peace or humanizing future wars **[page 66]** that is to say, banning the atomic bomb and disarmament, failed because no consensus could be reached on the matter of punishment of states and individuals in case of violations of the agreements. The Soviet Union was prepared to allow an international control on its territory, but expressly refused extradition of Soviet citizens to an international court as well as recognition of international jurisdiction on Soviet affairs. There is no longer any hope for a consensus on these decisive questions. Also there is no longer any chance that a judicial world authority will be established at the UN based on Roosevelt's plan. But with this, the principles which Jackson, the trusted adviser to Roosevelt, built into the London Charter on aspects of international criminal law, and according to which war crimes trials have proceeded up to this day, have failed. They were

[233] In this speech at Fulton, Missouri, Churchill first coined and made reference to the "iron curtain."

abandoned by the victorious powers just when they would have been obliged to have these very principles apply to themselves. The defense at Nuremberg pointed out that the basic principle *nulla poena sine lege*[234] was compromised because criminal law according to the London Charter, was only established after the offence. On the other hand it had always been pointed out during the trial and in many articles on this subject that this shortcoming had now been corrected and that since the Nuremberg trial, international legal order has been established on the basis of the London Charter which will be shaped within the framework of the UN. Just the opposite has happened. The London Charter has been abandoned and remains a one time and singular element of partisan activity on the part of the victors after the end of a war.

[page 67] Even if no new international law has been established *pro futuro*[235] as a consequence of Nuremberg, one could find consolation in the fact that during the course of handing out punishment for war crimes, existing international law has been strengthened and given new authority. How does it look now? Up to now international criminal law has been formally codified in the Hague Convention. The London Charter does not even mention the Hague Convention nor does it refer to it. Article 3: "Crimes against the customs and practices of war" is indeed concerned with pertinent activity. It has been formulated, however, to a special agenda and stretched to accommodate it. The formal judicial regulations of the Hague Convention have been completely ignored. The existing and internationally recognized institutions of the Hague were pushed aside and not applied. One signatory power of the London Charter also represented at the court had never joined the Hague Convention nor had it ever acknowledged it or kept to its regulations. The same is true for the Geneva

---

[234] The complete phrase, *nullem crimen, nulla poena sine lege,* means there can be no crime and no punishment without pre-existing law.

[235] "For the future."

Convention regarding prisoners of war.[236] At the trial the Hague Convention concerning land wars was quite regularly quoted, not as material procedural law, but rather *per analogiam*.[237] The defendants were reproached for each single violation of the Hague and Geneva Conventions. Wherever the victors themselves had disregarded conventions, as in unrestricted submarine warfare, in air raids against the civilian population and on targets of no military importance, in guerrilla warfare, in the deployment of commandos, etc. etc. there was tacit acceptance that the respective conventions were out of date. This turned out to be an advantage for one of the defendants in the case of submarine warfare, but not as far as the constituent law was concerned which remained weak with no punishment applicable for either side and was often referred to in the justification for sentencing. **[page 68]**

The applicable law had also been abandoned in the case of the temporal extension of the term war crimes, which in general terms was retroactive to the year 1933 and in some cases - Rosenberg, Streicher, the corps of political leaders - even to the time of the founding of the Party after 1918. The defense could lodge a formal objection that the Hitler regime had been recognized by all states, had established diplomatic relations until 1 September 1939 and with Russia and America for years during the war. They also objected to the fact that the contraventions of the Versailles Treaty had been recognized by the Great Powers in part before and in part after the proceedings, that the "criminal" rearmament of the Navy had occurred based on, and within the context of the London Naval Treaty with England,[238] that the *Anschluss*[239] of Austria had been recognized by all

[236] The Geneva Convention on the Treatment of Prisoners of War was signed in 1929 by all major countries except the Soviet Union.

[237] "As an analogy."

[238] The Anglo-German Naval Pact of 18 June 1935 was Britain's tacit recognition of Germany's right to revise the Versailles Treaty on naval matters. It allowed the Germans to build a navy 35 percent the size of the British navy and have parity in submarine strength.

[239] The *Anschluss* or union of Austria and Germany in March 1938 had been quickly

governments, etc. etc. The principle and *a priori*[240] impartiality of the Hague and Geneva Conventions had been clearly set aside.

For all these reasons we are justified in stating that the Nuremberg trial has not strengthened and revitalized international law pertaining to warfare. It has rather set it aside. This was also expressed in various debates at the United Nations and is confirmed by the fact that wars are being waged today in China, Thailand, Indonesia, Palestine and Greece in which the Hague and Geneva Conventions are not being followed. Also the Hague's mandatory required arbitration has not been invoked at all for settlement of these wars. **[page 69]** For this reason even the United Nations has not set in motion any judicial or arbitration machinery and has not proceeded beyond diplomatic wrangling, although millions of soldiers are fighting each other on the battlefield. This is enough to prove that the law of the past is no longer valid, that new law has not come into being and that therefore internationally there is currently no valid law.

I do not maintain that the Nuremberg trial alone can be blamed for this state of affairs. One can see how this negative pattern has been developing since the end of the First World War. All the efforts to strengthen and develop international law have failed, being consciously or unconsciously linked to imperialistic and intolerant ideas of world domination. Only by respecting national sovereignty can a new international law be reconstructed and only on the basis of a very realistic view of the world and its driving forces. In this war none of the warring parties has shown much respect for the applicable laws of war and no government may pose as judge over the other in this respect. But the London Charter, the Nuremberg trial and the other trials together with the international conferences and the new wars only now make clear to the whole world that the day has passed when legal relations between countries can be regulated by treaty,

---

recognized by the major states. Only a few smaller countries like Mexico had protested.

[240] Proceeding from the cause to the effect, from the antecedent to the consequence.

and that the 20th century has reverted to primitive times when the law is based on the power of the strong over the weak.

The stronger party should at least keep to the general norms of international law in fulfilling its role as judge and thus, though not possessing a formal right, at least has a moral right to act in this capacity. **[page 70]** The most general principle of any jurisdiction is that a judge must himself be free of all guilt. He himself must not have committed crimes of which he accuses somebody else. He must not punish where he himself would deserve punishment. Nor must a judge take personal revenge. One person can not be at the same time judge and avenger. According to these principles no warring state today has judicial authority. Having been defeated and convicted I am not entitled to accuse anybody, and thus refrain from presenting examples.[241] Instead I quote two items from the American army newspaper "Stars and Stripes" which I have personally translated. (The English text is available on demand.) "Stars and Stripes" of 19 September 1946: "Shaw maintains that A-Bombers are not qualified to condemn Nazi leaders. London, September 18 (AP).[sic] G. B. Shaw thinks that the allies have no moral right to condemn the Nazi defendants who await sentencing from the International Military Court in Nuremberg. "The atom bombs have blown our moral sphere out of the courtroom," the 90-year-old philosopher-writer said yesterday in answer to a written question. "After using the bomb without warning and without demonstration and after a repeat of this which was unnecessary logically we are hardly in a moral position to hang anybody." In a written piece for the first time showing a slightly trembling hand Shaw added: "I agree with Dr. Inge." He was referring to more recent declarations **[page 71]** published in a London newspaper by Dr. W. R. Inge, well known as the former "brilliant dean" of St. Paul's Cathedral. - "The court," Dr. Inge summed up, "ought to publish a calm and well-documented declaration on the crimes and then set them (the Nazi

[241] Rainer obviously felt restrained by the *tu quoque* argument (i.e., you were doing it too).

defendants) free with the mark of Cain on their foreheads. Perhaps the butcher of the Jews and one or two others ought to be executed, but not the majority." Shaw notes that although he agrees in principle with Dr. Inge, he could "however not guarantee that the mark of Cain would be more merciful than the rope." Meanwhile the National Council of the Peace Pledge Union, a pacifist organization, among whose founders are some of Great Britain's prominent literary and artistic personalities, has issued a declaration stating that the death sentence for the Nuremberg prisoners "could not be justified on moral grounds." It would not serve any useful purpose, the declaration added.[242]

"The Stars and Stripes" of 25 September 1946, page 6: "Robeson lobbies for Anti-Lynch-Action." Washington, September 24th(UP). An Anti-Lynch Group, led by the singer Paul Robeson, yesterday informed President Truman that unless the government did something about mob violence he "could be sure that the Blacks would." Robeson was leading a delegation representing the American crusade to stop lynching. The President, as Robeson reports, took up a hard stance towards a number of items presented by the delegation. Robeson told the reporters that the President "did not like to hear" the assurance **[page 72]** of the delegation that there was only a small difference between the lynchings going on and the Nuremberg War Criminal Trials. "The President was strongly opposed to this," Robeson said, "and told us to back our homeland, and that Great Britain and America were the last refuge of freedom in the world." - "I opposed this saying that the British Empire had been one of the greatest enslavers of human beings in the world." Robeson said that he had told the President "the mood of the Blacks might change."[243]

[242] With minor exceptions Rainer's account is accurate to the original English.

Inge told the press that the response to his position was "positively murderous." One woman wrote warning him that she would pray every night for his death.

[243] Again, Rainer's translation is accurate to the original English.

Rainer was aware of racial incidents that occurred among US soldiers in Nuremberg during the trial. Racial incidents, including fights, multiplied after a black unit arrived in Nuremberg.

The current extradition practice is diametrically opposed to international custom up to now. Extradition treaties generally provide for criminals to be handed over to the state of which they are citizens. A country's own citizens are not extradited as a rule even in the case of crime, but rather they are placed before a court in their own country (for the maintenance of reciprocity). In the case of criminal prosecutions, the accused is extradited to the country where the crime occurred following the principle: *locus regit actum.*[244] This is provided for only in a few extradition treaties and then only where there is reciprocity. Those accused of political crimes are very rarely extradited to the country of origin. Extradition of one's own citizens for political crimes never happens, as far as I know. A few countries have expressly proclaimed the right of asylum for foreign citizens in the case of political crimes, such as Switzerland, England, the USA. The London Charter put the United States into an awkward position when the countries of the Eastern Block demanded extradition of their citizens **[page 73]** who had collaborated with the Germans. These people have been assembled in camps, designated as "displaced persons," and are treated very well, as long as they stand against Communism. The following devise worked to their advantage when Mrs. Roosevelt,[245] impressed by her experiences when visiting such camps in Germany, organized a lobby in the American Congress stressing the tradition of America as the land of freedom, etc. After that the President ordered that only those displaced persons who wished it be extradited.[246] Only the Nazis are still being extradited.

---

[244] In private international law, the rule that, when a legal transaction complies with the formalities required by the law of the country where it is done, it is also valid in the country where it is to be given effect, although by the law of that country other formalities are required.

[245] Eleanor Roosevelt, wife of the US president, visited Germany in February 1946 gathering impressions of the occupied land. She expressed considerable interest in whether the bulk of the German people were still Nazi minded; whether they must re-educate themselves under close supervision; whether the main hope for a democratic Germany rested with the working classes and trade unions; and whether there were many non-Communist trade union leaders who could inspire confidence of the people in the labor movement.

[246] There is no evidence of such an order by either Roosevelt or his successor, Harry Truman. Rainer may have heard a rumor or he may be reflecting a feeling among fellow detainees that there was such a directive.

This means that a universally valid principle of law is not being applied, but rather these matters are being handled from the political perspective of one side. It is clear that on this basis an international extradition order which the Nuremberg process would raise into the sphere of international law cannot possibly occur. The war criminals of the next war will, just as now, not be named and extradited according to international law, but according to the will of the victors.

In recognition of these consequences, for quite some time, the Soviet Union appears to have stopped extraditing war criminals and carrying out war crimes trials. While defending their right to exist before the international forum of the Security Council and Atomic Commission[247] the Soviets proclaimed the principle of national sovereignty for themselves, their allies, and all suppressed peoples on earth, and in so doing they have rendered an immense service to the world. It is a logical consequence of this action **[page 74]** that they are keeping to these principles in their own dealings, even where previous enemies are concerned. The Soviet Union obviously does not want to run the risk of being reproached for inconsistencies in their foreign policy on account of how they handle war criminals *per argumentum a minore ad maiorem.*[248] Apparently they are less interested in taking revenge on individuals than securing the future life of the Soviet peoples and their allies. These are the elements of a realistic and genuine political ideology which alone will be able to renew and humanize the relationships among peoples.

I think it is perfectly possible to punish war crimes without destroying international law and to use the existing Hague Conventions with certain additions (which countries undertake freely or under compulsion of the peace treaty). This can be accomplished with international supervision. For an outsider

---

[247] The United Nation's Security Council and the Atomic Energy Commission.

[248] "By an argument of the lesser to the greater."

it is only the results of war that leads to decisions regarding political blocs. In the place of a judgment there is the peace treaty. As we have been taught by history the people usually know what to do with their leaders and demagogues. Interestingly, during the Nuremberg process, there was an attempt made to proclaim the international military court as a quasi German Supreme Court.[249] Discussing the Court's competence the French prosecutor de Menthon explained that in consequence of the unconditional surrender, the sovereignty of the government of the Reich had passed to the International Control Council which as chief magistrate, had transferred judicial power to the Nuremberg tribunal. **[page 75]** To this the German Professor of International Law Jareiss [sic] replied that in these circumstances German law must be applied. The court itself derived its authority only from the London Charter.

As far as we can see there will always be wars. It will not be fear of a war crimes trial that holds a patriot back from fighting for his country if its existence is threatened. Since the previous international law no longer exists and a new one has not yet been created each country will fight with everything at its disposal, for only victory will decide whether or not its military campaign was a crime. "Small wars" like those presently underway are manipulated by powerful patrons and are treated as a trifling matter. But if they themselves become involved it becomes a matter of life or death, using all possible means and facing every consequence. In the newspapers of both blocs one can already recognize the elements of the war crimes trials which will be followed. The far-reaching consequences of a future major war in a completely lawless international sphere, obviously makes responsible statesmen hesitate. Therein lies, perhaps, the only success during Mr. Jackson's tenure, which he did win willingly but as *advocatus diaboli.*[250]

---

[249] Among others, this was a suggestion made by Francois de Menthon in his opening speech.

[250] The "devil's advocate" originally described an official who argued against another's beatification or canonization.

Summing up I list here the most important principles on which an international criminal law could come into effect by treaty:

1.) only existing and recognized law is valid

2.) war crimes are only those actions which existing law describes as such,

3.) only neutral judges can pass judgment **[page 76]**

4.) the proceedings assure the prosecution and defense the same rights and privileges

5.) the principle of reciprocity is applicable

6.) the country where the convicted individual has citizenship is responsible for carrying out the sentence. This is overseen internationally. The defeated are charged with this responsibility in the peace treaty. The victor carries out such sentences voluntarily by order of parliament to fulfill his treaty obligations.

The effect of such an international agreement would be considerably strengthened, if the treaty partners were to include formal and substantive international criminal law as an essential component of their civil and military criminal law. The guiding principles could also be incorporated into the constitution.

Rainer's sketch of the Nuremberg Palace of Justice and Trial Room

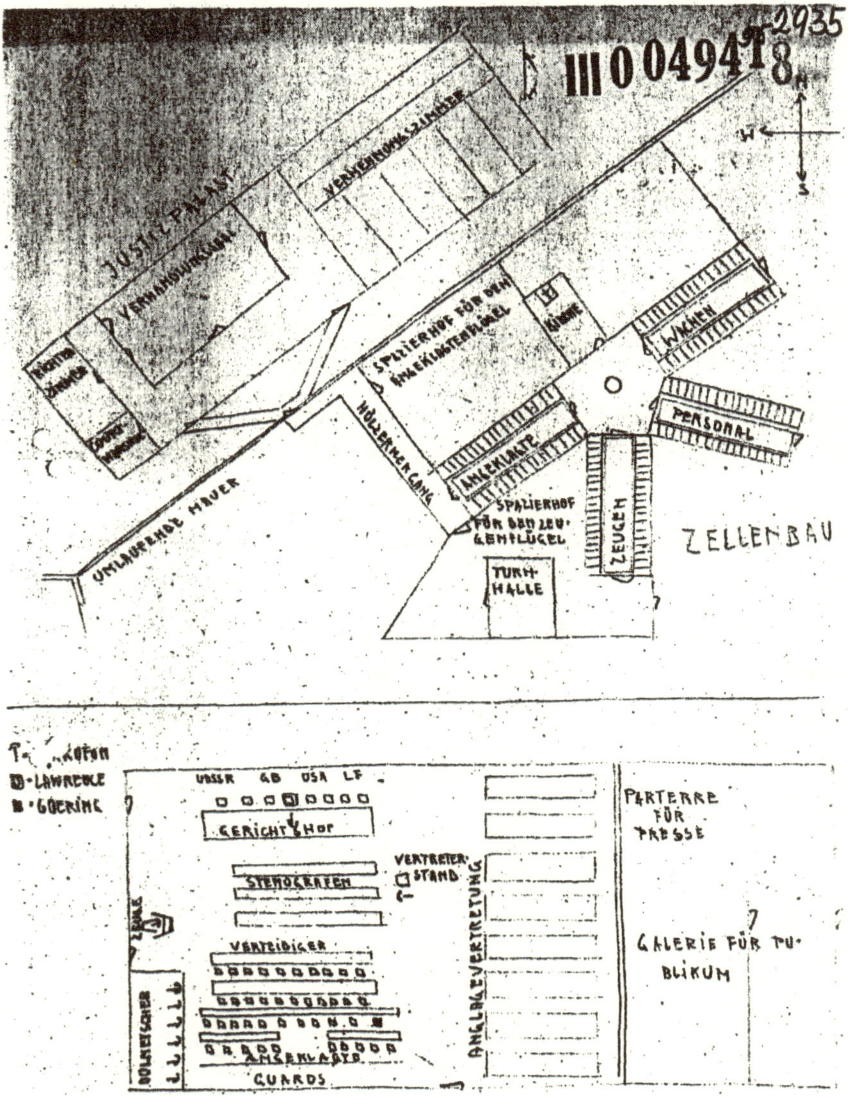

[Guide to symbols and words used on Rainer's sketch]

Map: W=W, N=N, O=E, S=S

Justizpalast:	Palace of Justice
Richterzimmer:	Judges' Room
Court Marshall	
Verhandlungssaal:	court room
Vernehmungszimmer:	interrogation room
umlaufende Mauer:	surrounding wall
Hölzerner Gang:	wooden corridor
Spazierhof für den Angeklagtenflügel:	walking courtyard for the defendants' wing
Kirche:	church
Angeklagte:	defendants
Wachen:	guards
Personal:	staff
Zeugen:	witnesses
Spazierhof für den Zeugenflügel:	walking courtyard for the witnesses' wing
Turnhalle:	gymnasium
Zellenbau:	cell building
Mikrofon:	microphone
Gerichtshof:	court
Stenografen:	stenographers
Vertreterstand:	representatives' stand
Verteidiger:	counsel for the defense
Zeuge:	witness
Dolmetscher:	interpreters
Angeklagte:	defendants
Guards	guards

Anglagevertretung [sic] [Anklagevertretung]:	counsel for the prosecution
Parterre für Presse:	balcony for the press
Galerie für Publikum:	gallery for spectators

Photo 1: Friedrich Rainer (1903 – 1950?).
Photo Collection Erwin Lerner, New York

THE INTERNATIONAL MILITARY TRIBUNAL

Defendant's Application for Summons for Witness

To: The General Secretary, The International Military Tribunal:

I, A. Seyss - Inquart (Name of Defendant), hereby request that the following person be summoned by the Tribunal to give evidence in my behalf:

Dr. Friedrich Reiner
(Name of Person Desired as Witness)

former Governor of Carinthia, perhaps in Nuremberg prison
(Occupation and Last Known Location)

OTHER INFORMATION THAT MAY AID IN LOCATING THE PERSON NAMED:

The person above named has knowledge of the following facts:

1) Has been currently oriented about my political intentions and plans.

2) Conversation in the train in the evening of 18 February. I do orient Dr. Reiner about the contents of my talk with Hitler as represented in the documents.

3) My standing aloof from the political situation on 11 March 1939 beginning with 1600 in the afternoon.

These facts are relevant to my defense for the following reasons:

My political plan was, that the Austrian National Socialists should receive permission to take an active part and share responsibility in the State, but this on account of an express declaration by Hitler as a Party Leader that the Austrian Party should stand upon the basis of the Austrian State and be completely independent from the Reich Party. These were also my demands from Hitler on the 17th of February. Therefore, the reproach of my participation in the conspiracy against Austrian independence becomes nullified. Further, beginning about 1600 on 11 March, no more influence upon the political developments.

6. Nov. 1945
(Date)

(signed) A. Seyss - Inquart
(Signature of Defendant)

Signature illegible
(Signature of Defendant's Counsel)

Photo 2: Seyss-Inquart's request for Rainer to appear as his witness at Nuremberg.
Ian Sayer Archive, Sunningdale, Berks, United Kingdom

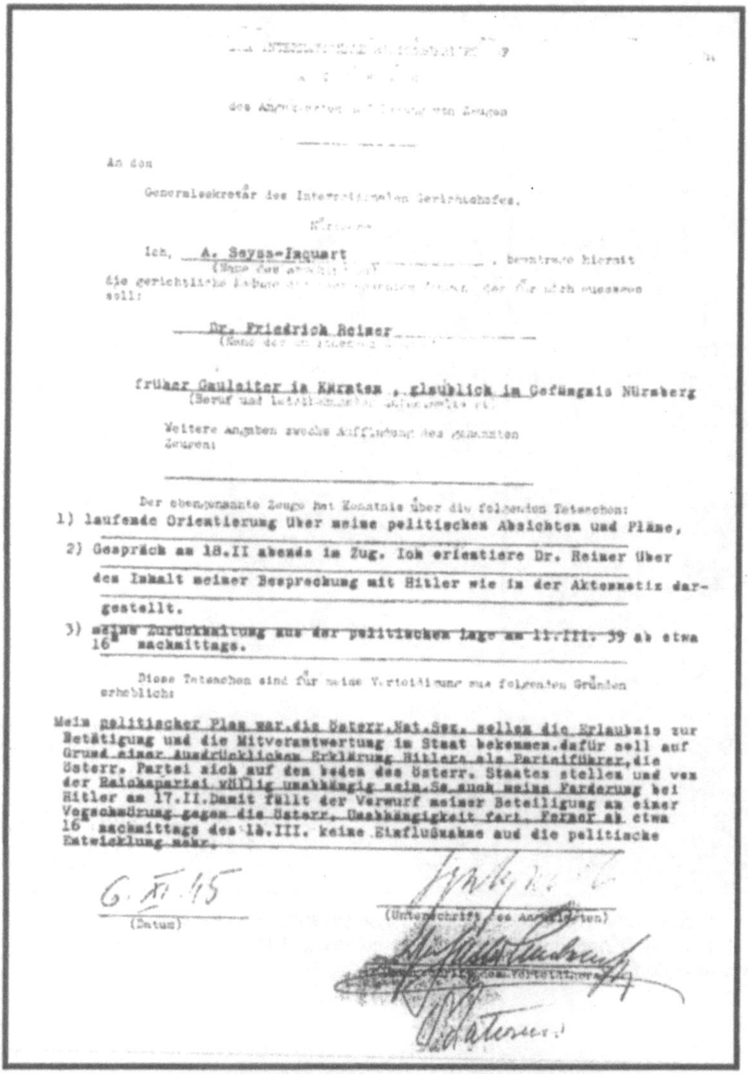

[illegible]

des Angeklagten [illegible] von Zeugen

An den

Generalsekretär des Internationalen Gerichtshofes,

Nürnberg

Ich, A. Seyss-Inquart (Name des Angeklagten), beantrage hiermit die gerichtliche Ladung des [illegible] Zeugen, der für mich aussagen soll:

Dr. Friedrich Rainer
(Name des [illegible] Zeugen)

früher Gauleiter in Kärnten , glaublich im Gefängnis Nürnberg
(Beruf und letzt[illegible])

Weitere Angaben zwecks Auffindung des genannten Zeugen:

Der obengenannte Zeuge hat Kenntnis über die folgenden Tatsachen:

1) laufende Orientierung über meine politischen Absichten und Pläne,

2) Gespräch am 18.II abends im Zug. Ich orientiere Dr. Rainer über den Inhalt meiner Besprechung mit Hitler wie in der Aktennotiz dargestellt.

3) meine Zurückhaltung aus der politischen Lage am 11.III. 39 ab etwa 16[h] nachmittags.

Diese Tatsachen sind für meine Verteidigung aus folgenden Gründen erheblich:

Mein politischer Plan war, die Österr. Nat. Soz. sollen die Erlaubnis zur Betätigung und die Mitverantwortung im Staat bekommen, dafür soll auf Grund einer ausdrücklichen Erklärung Hitlers als Parteiführer, die Österr. Partei sich auf den Boden des Österr. Staates stellen und von der Reichspartei völlig unabhängig sein. So auch meine Forderung bei Hitler am 17.II. Damit fällt der Vorwurf meiner Beteiligung an einer Verschwörung gegen die Österr. Unabhängigkeit fort. Ferner ab etwa 16 nachmittags des 11.III. keine Einflußnahme auf die politische Entwicklung mehr.

6. XI. 45
(Datum)

(Unterschrift des Angeklagten)

Photo 3: The German language original request for Rainer to appear at Nuremberg.
Ian Sayer Archive, Sunningdale, Berks, United Kingdom

Photo 4: Aerial view of Palace of Justice and prison, Nuremberg.
Photo Collection Ray D'Addario, Holyoke, Massachusetts, and The Robert H. Jackson Center, Jamestown, New York

Photo 5: The Palace of Justice, Nuremberg, site of the International Military Tribunal.
Ian Sayer Photo Archive, Sunningdale, Berks, United Kingdom

Photo 6: A guard and his light keeping close watch on a defendant.
Ian Sayer Photo Archive, Sunningdale, Berks, United Kingdom

Photo 7: A typical cell in the Nuremberg prison.
Photo Collection Ray D'Addario, Holyoke, Massachusetts, and The Robert H. Jackson Center, Jamestown, New York

Photo 8: An unknown detainee's sketch of a Nuremberg prison cell.
Ian Sayer Archive, Sunningdale, Berks, United Kingdom

HEADQUARTERS
INTERNAL SECURITY DETACHMENT
OFFICE, U. S. CHIEF OF COUNSEL
APO 403, U. S. ARMY

19 October 1945

ROSTER, WITH HOUR INDICTMENT WAS SERVED

CELL NUMBER	INTERNEE	TIME SERVED
4	HESS, R.	1343—1347
5	GOERING, H.	1348—1352
6	JODL, A.	1353—1358
7	RIBBENTROP, J.	1359—1404
8	KEITEL, W.	1406—1415
9	LEY, R.	1416—1421
10	von NEURATH, C.	1423—1428
11	SAUCKEL, F.	1429—1435
12	von Papen, F.	1436—1441
13	DOENITZ, K.	1442—1447
14	SEYSS-INQUART, A.	1448—1454
15	FRANK, H.	1455—1503
16	ROSENBERG, A.	1504—1509
18	FUNK, W.	1510—1517
19	FRICK, W.	1519—1526
20	SPEER, A.	1527—1534
23	SHIRACH, B.	1535—1540
24	SCHACHT, H.	1541—1549
25	STREICHER, J.	1550—1559
26	KALTENBRUNNER, E.	1600-1608

von Bohlen, Fritzsche, Raeder, and Bormann not yet joined.

B. C. ANDRUS
Colonel, Cav
Commandant.

Photo 9: Colonel Andrus' roster of when the indictments were served.
Ian Sayer Archive, Sunningdale, Berks, United Kingdom

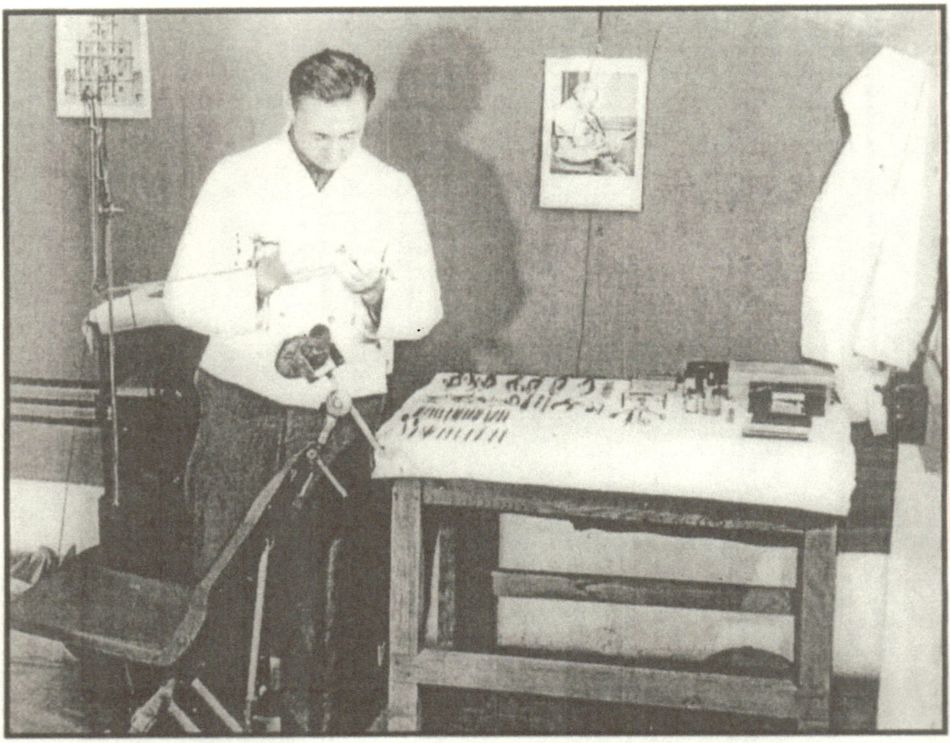

Photo 10: Nuremberg's dentist, Dr. Heinz Hoch, preparing for another patient.
Ian Sayer Photo Archive, Sunningdale, Berks, United Kingdom

Photo 11: Dr. Ludwig Pflücker, German Prisoner of War and resident physician to the defendants and detainees, working at his desk.
Ian Sayer Photo Archive, Sunningdale, Berks, United Kingdom

Photo 12: The prison barber returning razor blades at the end of the day.
Ian Sayer Photo Archive, Sunningdale, Berks, United Kingdom

Photo 13: Protestant Pastor Henry Gerecke in his chapel, a converted cell.
Photo Collection Ray D'Addario, Holyoke, Massachusetts, and The Robert H. Jackson Center, Jamestown, New York

Photo 14: Prisoners walking under the watchful eye of the guards in the exercise yard at Nuremberg.
Ian Sayer Photo Archive, Sunningdale, Berks, United Kingdom

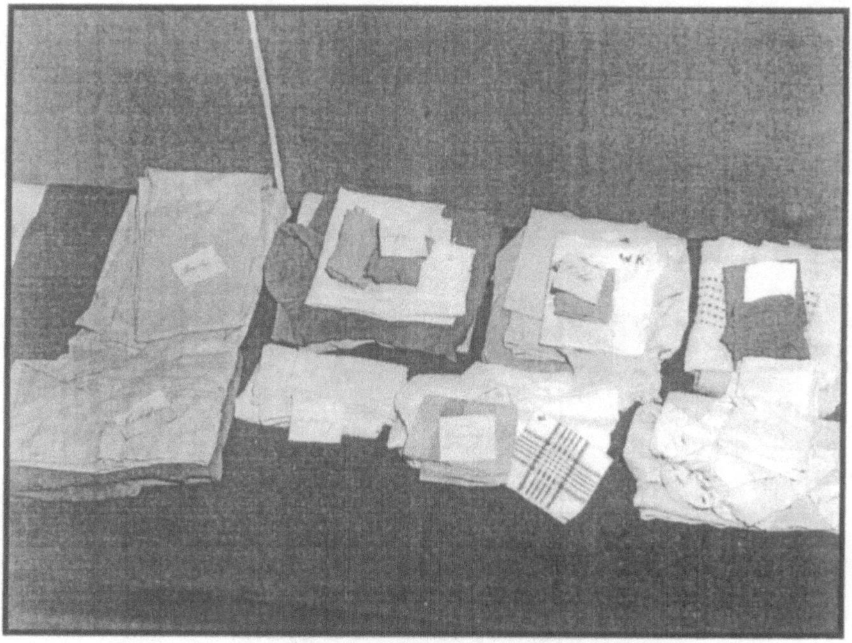

Photo 15: One of the small comforts at Nuremberg: clean clothes.
Ian Sayer Photo Archive, Sunningdale, Berks, United Kingdom

Photo 16: The signing of the London Charter, July 1945. Left to right: A. N. Trainin (USSR), General I. T. Nikitchenko (USSR), the Lord Chancellor, Lord Jowitt (UK), Robert Jackson (USA), and M. Falco (France).
Ian Sayer Photo Archive, Sunningdale, Berks, United Kingdom

Photo 17: The defendants in court. Rainer's comrade, Seyss-Inquart, is in the second row, fourth from the right, between Papen and Speer.
Photo Collection Ray D'Addario, Holyoke, Massachusetts, and The Robert H. Jackson Center, Jamestown, New York

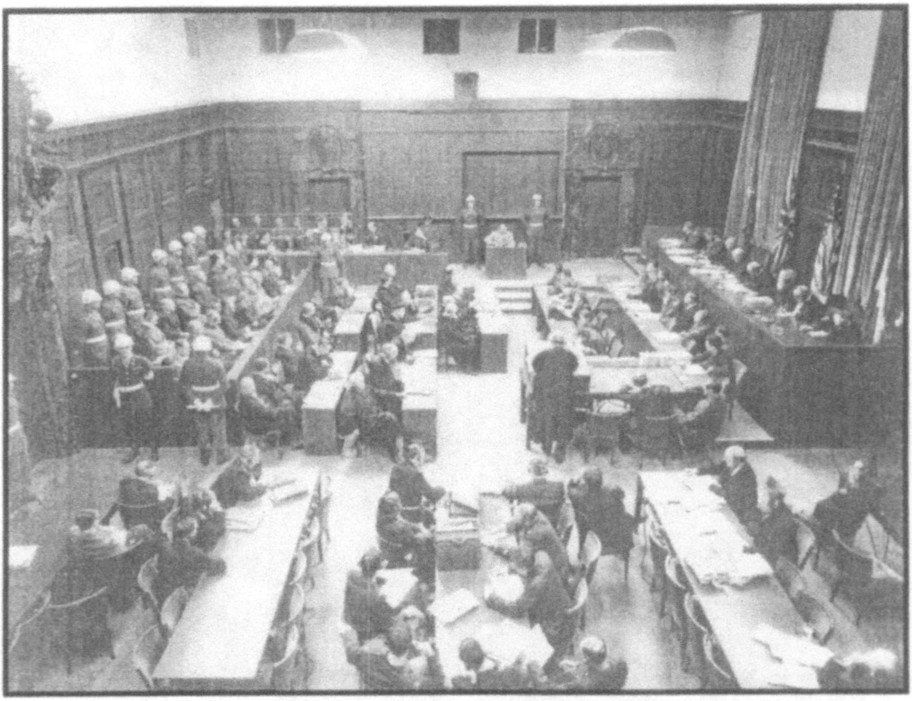

Photo 18: The International Military Tribunal courtroom during the examination of Göring.
Ian Sayer Photo Archive, Sunningdale, Berks, United Kingdom

Photo 19: Lord Justice Geoffrey Lawrence. Sitting next to him is Francis Biddle (US).
Ian Sayer Photo Archive, Sunningdale, Berks, United Kingdom

Photo 20: The press gallery, IMT courtroom.
Ian Sayer Photo Archive, Sunningdale, Berks, United Kingdom

Photo 21: Some of the defence lawyers and associates at Nuremberg. Left to right, first row: Egon Kubuschok (Papen), Robert Servatius (Sauckel), Alfred Seidl (Frank), Hanns Marx (Streicher); second row: Franz Exner (Jodl), Fritz Sauter (Funk), Otto Stahmer (Göring), Walter Ballas, Hans Flächsner (Speer), Gunthner von Rohrscheidt (Hess); third row: Georg Fröschmann (Associate, Ribbentrop), Heinz Fritz (Fritzsche), Otto Pannenbecher (Frick), Alfred Thoma (Rosenberg), Kurt Kaufman (Kaltenbrunner), Hans Laternser (Associate, Seyss-Inquart).

Ian Sayer Photo Archive, Sunningdale, Berks, United Kingdom

Photo 22: Gustav Steinbauer, Seyss-Inquart's lawyer.
Photo Collection Ray D'Addario, Holyoke, Massachusetts, and The Robert H. Jackson Center, Jamestown, New York

Photo 23: A typical lawyer and defendant meeting. Papers were examined first by the guard to ensure there were no concealed weapons.
Ian Sayer Photo Archive, Sunningdale, Berks, United Kingdom

Photo 24: Rainer's old comrade, Arthur Seyss-Inquart, who was convicted and executed at Nuremberg.
Ian Sayer Photo Archive, Sunningdale, Berks, United Kingdom

Photo 25: Seyss-Inquart returning from lunch.
Photo Collection Ray D'Addario, Holyoke, Massachusetts, and The Robert H. Jackson Center, Jamestown, New York

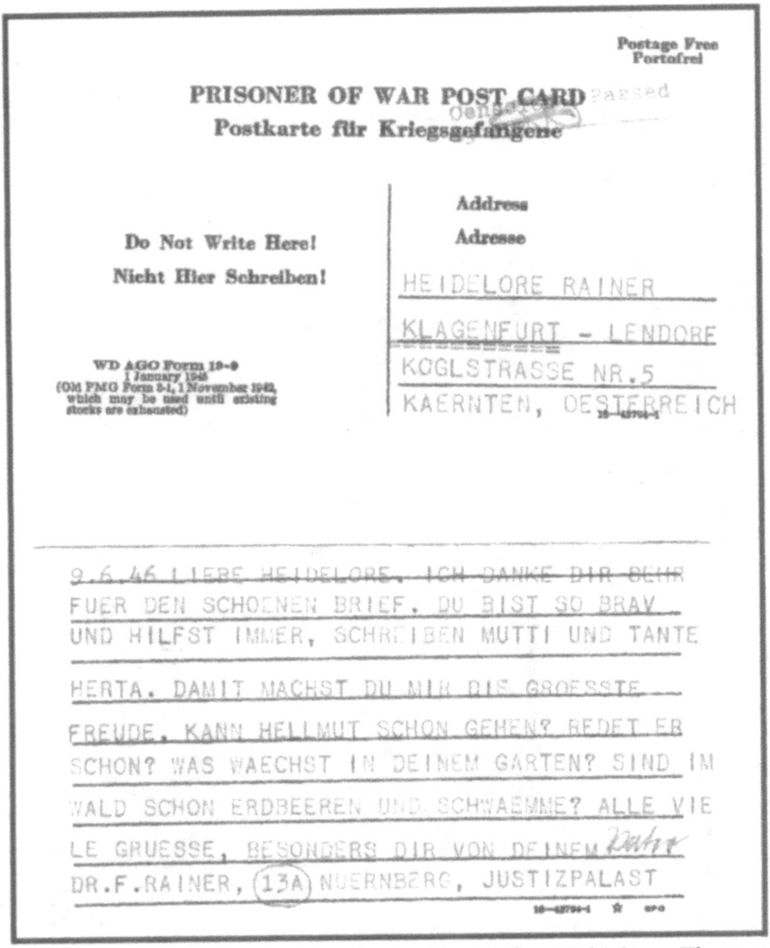

Postage Free
Portofrei

PRISONER OF WAR POST CARD
Postkarte für Kriegsgefangene

Do Not Write Here!
Nicht Hier Schreiben!

WD AGO Form 19-9
1 January 1945
(OM PMG Form 8-1, 1 November 1942, which may be used until existing stocks are exhausted)

Address
Adresse

HEIDELORE RAINER
KLAGENFURT - LENDORF
KOGLSTRASSE NR.5
KAERNTEN, OESTERREICH

9.6.46 LIEBE HEIDELORE. ICH DANKE DIR SEHR
FUER DEN SCHOENEN BRIEF. DU BIST SO BRAV
UND HILFST IMMER, SCHREIBEN MUTTI UND TANTE
HERTA. DAMIT MACHST DU MIR DIE GROESSTE
FREUDE. KANN HELLMUT SCHON GEHEN? REDET ER
SCHON? WAS WAECHST IN DEINEM GARTEN? SIND IM
WALD SCHON ERDBEEREN UND SCHWAEMME? ALLE VIE
LE GRUESSE, BESONDERS DIR VON DEINEM Vater
DR.F.RAINER, (13A) NUERNBERG, JUSTIZPALAST

Photo 26: A POW post card: Rainer to his daughter Heidelore. The text reads: Dear Heidelore. Thank you very much for your lovely letter. Mother and Aunt Herta write that you are so good and helpful. That gives me great pleasure. Can Hellmut walk yet? Does he talk yet? What is growing in your garden? Are there strawberries and mushrooms in the woods yet? Many greetings to everyone, especially to you from your father.

Rainer Family Collection, Klagenfurt, Austria

APPENDICES

HEADQUARTERS
INTERNAL SECURITY DETACHMENT
OFFICE, U. S. CHIEF OF COUNSEL
APO 403, U.S. ARMY

2 September 1945

STEPS TAKEN TO PREPARE FOR CONFINEMENT OF THE WAR CRIMINALS

1. Iron hooks and projects removed from all cells.

2. Replacement of all glass window panes with cello-glass.

3. Removal of all weapons or instruments which might be used for suicide or self harm completed for each prisoner upon his arrival.

4. German doctor on duty in cell block 24 hours per day. (40 years professional practice) Treatment prescribed by American army doctor who visits internees daily.

5. Dentist provided in the cell block. All dental work kept up to date. Equipment and training permits every care except construction of dentures.

6. Equipment adequate for all First Aid nearby. An Army dispensary with complete medicines available on call in three minutes.

7. All meals prepared in the cell block under US Army standards of sanitation by German prisoners of war interned for that purpose. All expert cooks brought from Mondorf. Meals served to internees in their cells, in US Army meat cans and canteen cups without handles, and only a spoon with no (repeat no) knife or fork. Food passed in under supervision of sentinel and dishes passed out under supervision of sentinel to prevent communication and passage of contrabands, including notes.

8. Fresh canteen cup full of treated drinking water kept in each cell throughout the day and replenished periodically under supervision of a guard.

9. Each cell contains a sanitary flush toilet, straw mattress and plenty of blankets. Prisoners are provided woolen stockings. Felt boots are provided in case trials extend into severely cold weather.

10. Each cell contains a flimsey [sic] table not capable of being stood upon. All internees are provided with all the writing paper and pencils they desire and are encouraged to write. They write letters to their relatives which in all cases are forwarded to proper authority requesting posting. They write letters to the Commandant and to the Chief of Counsel [sic] Much of this has interrogation value and is promptly sent to the chief of interrogation.

11. German speaking American Army Chaplains of Evangelical Lutheran and of Roman Catholic faith minister to the spiritual needs of the prisoners.

12. Ports in the cell doors are kept open at all times. Sentinels moving back and forth on the catwalks view the prisoners every half minute for the purpose of preventing attempted suicide or other mischief.

13. Insecticide is employed in the cell block to prevent ingress of vermen [sic] and parasites from other parts of the prison.

14. Laundry is done in the prison laundry, carefully inspected for sanitation on return and if repairs are needed this is done by the prisoner of war brought from Mondorf for this purpose [sic] (In addition to his other duties).

15. Twice a week the route to the prison showers is guarded off and all prisoners in our wing are conducted there for a hot bath.

16. Prisoners are shaved daily by a trusted prisoner of war barber brought from Mondorf who shaves them under guard with a safety razor. No conversation is permitted between the barber and the internee prisoner. Upon completion of his task each day he turns in to the Prison Office the razor blades which were inventoried out to him at the start of his task.

17. No communication is permitted between internees nor between them and anyone except their immediate custodians, chaplains and interrogators.

18. The most rigid adherance [sic] to prison discipline and to courtesy and proper bearing is demanded of all prisoners.

19. The lighting system was completely altered to prevent suicide.

20. Repair to roof and skylight was made.

21. Boarding up of cell block to wall it off from the rest of the prison was necessary.

22. Wire mesh on catwalks was installed to prevent suicide leaps.

23. Plastering of cells to repair damage caused to walls by the removal of brackets and other projections.

24. Runways to offices and court house completed to prevent being viewed by those not concerned.

25. Arms in the cell block. The assistant prison officer and warden are provided with Thompson sub-machine guns kept in the Prison Office for emergency. The guard reserve is provided with pistols for emergency. The sentinels posted at the entrance to the cell block are armed with pistols and blackjacks. Sentinels on the catwalks and those required to enter the cells (accompanying the barber, doctor [sic] etc) are armed with blackjacks.

[page break]

25. (Continued) Sentinels outside the cell block within the prison are armed with Thompson sub-machine guns and pistols. Escort sentinels taking prisoners outside of the prison to interrogation or to the court are armed with pistols and handcuffs.

26. Eye glasses were removed from prisoners upon confinement. These are issued for use in the day time but taken in again before dark.

[Signature]
B. C. ANDRUS
Colonel, Cav
Commandant

SOURCE: USNA, RG 238, Correspondence, etc. of 6850th Internal Security Detachment, 1945-1949, Box 39, Folder: Prisoners of War

HEADQUARTERS
INTERNAL SEUCRITY [sic] DETACHMENT
OFFICE, U. S. CHIEF OF COUNSEL
APO 403, U.S. ARMY

11 September 1945

RULES FOR PRISONERS

DEFINITIONS:

a. Internee: The word internee in these regulations will be understood to include all persons confined here who are not required to perform labor or other duties with respect to prison operations.

b. Prisoner: The term prisoner applies to all persons confined here.

c. Prisoner of War: The term prisoner of war will be understood to include all medical, clerical, and labor personnel confined here for the purpose of operating this prison.

1. Internees are not allowed to talk with one another. They will not attempt in any way to communicate with one another, nor with anyone else except as listed in a, b, c, and d:

a. Internees are not allowed to talk to guards nor prisoners of war except in the line of duty.

b. They may write to their families, to the commandant, interrogators and legal authorities, only through the Prison Office.

c. Prisoners may converse freely with the Commandant, Prison Officer, Assistant Prison Officers, Wardens, doctors, dentists, and spiritual advisors on any matters pertaining to the office of those individuals.

d. Conversations will be conducted through an interpreter when necessary.

2. No internee will attempt to pass contraband articles to any person nor accept contraband articles sent to him by any person.

3. Guards will check the meal trays to see that no contraband articles are being passed to or from the internees and that all utensils are accounted for.

4. (Not for publication)

5. The German doctor will see each internee daily. An American Interpreter will accompany the doctor. Need for dental work should be mentioned at that time.

6. Cutting of hair, shaving etc, will be done by the German barber accompanied by an American Guard. No conversations are permitted.

7. Internees will ba [sic] allowed two shower baths per week.

[page break]

RULES FOR PRISONERS, dtd 11 September 1945, Headquarters, Internal Security Detachment, Office, US Chief of Counsel,

8. Reading and writing:

a. Bibles will be provided for all internees desiring them.

b. German books may be obtained from the prison office on request to the interpreter or members of the prison staff. A list of books will be made available from which selections may be made. Books will be returned after a reasonable time to permit circulation.

c. Writing materials will be provided in any quantity desired.

d. Number of letters and postcards authorized for personal communication to families will be announced from time to time. Delivery cannot be assured until the German Postal System is fully operating.

9. Internees will be responsible for the cleanliness of their respective cells. Necessary materials for this purpose will be brought to internees' cells.[sic]daily.

10. Internees will be exercised daily, the following rules applying:

a. Internees will be exercised more than one at a time.

b. They will not approach each other closer than 10 meters.

c. The internee may walk anywhere in the yard but not closer to the building or wall than the outer edge of the sidewalk or driveway.

d. Internees will not pickup anything or sit down.

e. Internees will not speak or signal anyone except the sentry [sic] then only in the line of duty.

11. Complaints regarding prison policies etc., will be in writing and addressed to the Commandant.

12. Formalities and Courtesies:
While it is not intended to go into great detail as to matters of common courtesy, the following five (5) rules are now published for compliance. These will serve as a guide to anyone under circumstances not specifically covered. In case of doubt it is best to err on the side of formality:

a. Exchange of Military Salutes between prisoners and allied personnel having been prohibited, the universal courtesy of bowing is deemed and [sic] appropriate substitution between internees and allied officers.

b. All allied personnel will take presedence [sic] in passing a doorway, a hall, stair or any other passage. Internees and prisoners will stand aside when approaching such places simutaneously [sic] with allied personnel.

[page break]

RULES FOR PRISONERS, dtd 11 September 1945, Headquarters, Internal Security Detachment, Office, US Chief of Counsel

12. Formalities and Courtesies: (Continued)

c. When allied officers, civilian dignitaries, or visiting inspectors enter a room or apartment occupied by internees, the internees will arise and remain standing at attention facing the allied representative until directed to do otherwise, (except that patients in bed or in sick chairs will remain in position, [sic] be silent, and give their attention to the visitor awaiting initial word from him for any conversation desired.

d. Prisoners marching through corridors or runways will halt and stand at attention for the Commandant, the Executive Officer, and all visiting dignitaries, either military or civilian, when they approach to pass. Those exercising in the yard will halt and face the Commandant or the Executive Officer when they enter, awaiting release by them before continuing exercising.

e. In all these cases if the Commandant or distinguished persons remain in the vicinity, upon this courtesy being acknowledged by a bow from them, the internees are released to continue their activity.

[Signature]
B. C. ANDRUS
Colonel, Cav
Commandant

SOURCE: USNA, RG238, Correspondence, etc. of 6850th Internal Security Detachment, 1945-1949, Box 39, Folder: Prisoners of War

HEADQUARTERS

6850TH INTERNAL SECURITY DETACHMENT

INTERNATIONAL MILITARY TRIBUNAL

10 November 1945

Subject: Prisoner Routine, Nurnberg [sic] Jail

To: Personnel Concerned

1. The prisoners are awakened each morning shortly before breakfast by the noise of the changing Guard.

2. Before breakfast is served, fresh water for washing purposes is brought and the old water disposed of by trusted P.W. Labor.

3. Breakfast is served at 0700 hours by a P.W. laborer from the kitchen who passes the food through the port in the door in a U.S. Army Meat Can with one piece of silverware, a<u>SPOON</u> [sic], and the drink for that meal is served in an Army Canteen Cup without a handle. When meat or other food which requires a knife is served, it is so prepared in the kitchen that it can be eaten with a spoon. After the Prisoner has finished with his meal, the attendant returns and gets the empty Mess Kit, making sure that every piece is returned.

4. Soon after breakfast, another P.W. laborer brings a broom and mop so that the Prisoner can clean his cell. (Each prisoner is responsible for keeping his own cell clean.)

5. Next a P.W. laborer brings fresh (chlorinated) drinking water, or on very cold days, mid-morning coffee is served.

6. After this comes the barber who shaves each Prisoner with a safety razor. (The barber is responsible for every piece of his equipment including all old blades). At no time are conversations allowed between the German P.W.s and the Prisoners. And, at all times every occurrance [sic] is under the supervision of an American Soldier Guard.

7. During the morning or afternoon the German Doctor comes for his checkup. Should a Prisoner need medical care, he is taken to the dispensary where he receives treatment. Or should he need dental treatment, he is escorted to the Dental Clinic in the Prison where a German Dentist administers to his ailment. All of this is under the supervision of a Guard. In addition to the medical and dental care given by the German Doctors, an American Army Doctor is on duty at all times in the Prison, and this doctor views each Prisoner once each day.

8. At noon the food is brought and served in the same manner as at all other meals.

[page break]

SUBJECT: Prisoner Routine, Nurnberg [sic] Jail
MEMORANDUM: TO: Personnel Concerned Dtd 10 November 1945, Hq 6850th ISD

9. There are two U.S. Army Chaplains who speak German fluently, one of the Roman Catholic and the other Evangelical Lutheran faith who administer to each of the Prisoner's spiritual needs who desire them.

10. Each day according to the Prison Schedule each Prisoner receives 30 minutes of outdoor exercise.

11. On any day the Prisoner may be called for interrogation or for a conference with his counsel, which further break prison monotony.

12. At 1800 hours supper is served in the usual manner.

13. Also during the day the Prisoners may request a book from the Library or he may have a deck of cards or a game of chess, etc for self relaxation.

14. The Prison Officer also visits each Prisoner at least once every day to check on their comfort and well-being and to hear any gripes or complaints which may have arisen.

15. The Prisoners are permitted lights each evening until 2130 hours for reading purposes or for work on their defense. Heavy wire mesh is fastened to the cell door covering the port hole behind which a shaded light is suspended which shines into the cell.

16. Shower facilities are available in the prison. Each Prisoner is permitted one shower per week either on Tuesday or Friday evenings.

17. Laundry is picked up once each week, cleaned, pressed, and returned to the prisoner.

18. All of the above are provided and executed for the Prisoner's Mental and Physical health so as to prevent morbid depressions commonly found with prisoners in solitary confinement.

[Signature]
B. C. ANDRUS
Col. Cav.
Commanding

SOURCE: USNA, RG 238, Correspondence, etc. of 6850th Internal Security Detachment, 1945-1949, Box 8, Folder: Reference

SAMPLE MENUS, NUREMBERG

<u>Friday, 31 August 1945</u>

Breakfast: Bread and butter
Coffee
Lunch: Noodles-Soup with fresh meat
Bread

Supper: Sausage
Cheese
Bread and butter

<u>Thursday, 25 October 1945</u>

Breakfast: Oatmeal
Biscuits
Lunch: Noodle soup
Beef hash
Potatoes
Sauerkraut
Coffee

Supper: Peas
Scrambled eggs
Bread
Tea

<u>Tuesday, 25 December 1945</u>

Breakfast: Oatmeal
Bread
Lunch: Soup
Beef hash
Vegetables
Spaghetti
Coffee
Supper: Fish and bread
Tea

<u>Monday, 18 February 1946</u>

Breakfast: Oatmeal
Bread
Lunch: Beef hash
Potatoes
Sugar peas
Bread and coffee

Supper: Bread pudding
Plums & peaches
Bread and tea

<u>Sunday, 17 March 1946</u>

Breakfast: Bread and jam
Coffee

Lunch: Soup
Boiled beef
Potatoes
Beets salad
Scrambled eggs
Coffee

Supper: Cheese and butter
Bread and coffee

<u>Tuesday, 30 April 1946</u>

Breakfast: Sweet Soup

Lunch: Soup
Hash
Beets salad
Peas
Coffee

Supper: Beans
Scrambled eggs
Tomato-sauce
Bread and tea

Ed. note: All menus were in English and German. Each menu was signed at the bottom by Loescken while the initials BUU (?) were in the top right corner of each page.

SOURCE: USNA, RG 238, 6850 Internal Security, Box 2, Folder: Menus--Misc Books

BIBLIOGRAPHY

UNPUBLISHED SOURCES

Arhiv Republike Slovenije, Ljubljana
ARS-III Proces proti dr. Rainer, Inv 761
Arbeiterkammer, Vienna
Pressearchiv
Bundesarchiv, Berlin-Lichterfelde
Abt. R (formerly Berlin Document Center)
Personalakten: Odilo Globočnik, Friedrich Rainer
Pressearchiv (formerly Zentralarchiv Potsdam)
Bundesarchiv, Koblenz
Sammlung Schumacher 304
Hoover Institution Microfilm Collection, Stanford, California
NSDAP Hauptarchiv, Reel 6, Folder 143 - Kärnten
National Archives and Records Administration, College Park, Maryland
Microfilm: T 84, R 16
Politisches Archiv des Auswärtigen Amtes, Bonn
Handakten Megerle, Bd. NSDAP 5/5
Public Record Office (now The National Archives), London
WO 204/11505
FO 1007/300
FO 371/46682

INTERVIEWS

Magister Luba Dornik Šubelj, ARS-III, Ljubljana, Slovenia, 15.10.1996.

DOCUMENTARY SOURCES

Bard, Mitchell, ed. The Nuremberg Trial. San Diego: Greenhaven Press, 2002.

Diller, Ansgar, and Mühl-Benninghaus, Wolfgang, eds. Berichterstattung über den Nürnberger Prozess gegen die Haupkriegsverbsrecher 1945/46: Edition und Dokumentation ausgewählter Rundfunkquellen. [Herausgeber, Deutsches Rundfunkarchiv]. Potsdam: Verlag für Berlin-Brandenburg, 1998.

Friedman, Tuviah, ed. The Two Antisemitic Nazi-leaders: Alfred Rosenberg and Julius Streicher at the Nuremberg Trial 1946 / Documentary Collection by Tuviah Friedman. Haifa, Israel: Institute of Documentation in Israel for the Investigation of Nazi War Crimes, 1988.

Goldensohn, Leon. The Nuremberg Interviews / Conducted by Leon Goldensohn. Edited and Introduction by Robert Gellately. New York: Knopf, 2004.

Great Britain. Her Majesty's Stationary Office, International Military Tribunal. The Judgement of Nuremberg, 1946. London: Stationary Office, 1999.

International Military Tribunal. Trial of the Major War Criminals before the International Military Tribunal, Nuremberg, 14 November 1945 – 1 October 1946. 42 vols. Nuremberg: International Military Tribunal, 1947.

Jackson, Robert H. The Nürnberg Case as Presented by Robert H. Jackson, Chief of Counsel for the United States, together with Other Documents. New York: Cooper Square Publishers, 1971.

Marrus, Michael R. The Nuremberg War Crimes Trial 1945-46 – A Documentary History. New York: Bedford Books, 1977.

McMillan, James. Five Men at Nuremberg. London: Harrap, 1985.

Nazi Conspiracy and Aggression. 11 vols., 2 supplements. Washington, D.C.: Government Printing Office, 1946-1948.

Overy, Richard. Interrogations: The Nazi Elite in Allied Hands, 1945. New York: Viking, 2001.

Smith, Bradley F. The American Road to Nuremberg: The Documentary Record, 1944-1945. Stanford, Calif.: Hoover Institution Press, 1982.

Schonfeld, Walter T. Nazi Madness: Highlighted at Nuremberg. London: Minerva, 2000.

Stave, Bruce M., and Michele Palmer with Leslie Frank. Witnesses to Nuremberg: An Oral History of American Participants at the War Crimes Trials. New York: Twayne Publishers, 1998.

United Nations. Secretary General (1946-1953). The Charter and Judgment of the Nürnberg Tribunal, History and Analysis: Memorandum submitted by the Secretary General. Lake Success: UN, General Assembly, International Law Commission, 1949.

PERSONAL SOURCES

Amen, John Harlen. The Reminiscences of John H. Amen. Glen Rock: Microfilming Corporation of America, 1972.

Andrus, Burton C. I Was the Nuremberg Jailer. New York: Coward: McCann, 1969. (English edition titled: The Infamous of Nuremberg. London: Leslie Frewin, 1969.)

Biddle, Francis. In Brief Authority. Garden City, N.Y.: Doubleday, 1962.

Birkett, Norman. The Lessons of Nuremberg: Address delivered on August 20, 1947 in Hotel Vancouver, Vancouver, BC. Vancouver: Canadian Club of Vancouver, 1947.

Calvocoressi, Peter. Nuremberg: The Facts, the Law, and the Consequences. London: Chatto and Windus, 1947.

Cooper, R. W. The Nuremberg Trial. London: Penguin Books, 1947.

Dönitz, Karl. Memoirs: Ten Years and Twenty Days. London: Weidenfield and Nicolson, 1959. (Translation of Zehn Jahre und Zwanzig Tage.)

Elwyn-Jones, Frederick (Lord Elwyn-Jones). In My Time – An Autobiography. London: Weidenfeld and Nicolson, 1983.

Fritzsche, Hans. The Sword in the Scales; as told to Hildegard Springer. Translated by Diana Pike, Heinrich Fraenkel and Frank Owen. London: Alan Wingate, 1953.

Gaskin, Hilary, ed. Eyewitnesses at Nuremberg. London: Arms and Armour Press, 1990.

Gilbert, G. M. Nuremberg Diary. New York: Da Capo Press, 1995 (with the addition of 24 photographs from the 1961 edition).

Halan, Yaroslav. Reports from Nuremberg. Pamphlets. Trans. from Ukraine by Anatole Bilenko. Kiev: Dnipro Publishers, 1984.

Harris, Whitney R. Tyranny on Trial: The Evidence at Nuremberg. Rev. ed. Dallas: Southern Methodist University Press, 1999.

Kalnoky, Ingeborg. The Guest House: A Nuremberg Memoir of Countess Kalnoky, With Ilona Herisko. Indianopolis: Bobbs- Merrill Company, 1974.

Kilmuir, David Patrick Maxwell-Fyfe, Earl of. Political Adventure; the Memoirs of the Earl of Kilmuir. London: Weidenfeld and Nicolson, 1964.

Keitel, Wilhelm. The Memoirs of Field-Marshal Keitel. Walter Görlitz, ed. Trans. by David Irving. Originally published 1966. New York: Cooper Square Publishers, 2000. (German original: Mein Leben; Pflichterfüllung bis zum Untergang: Hitler Feldmarschall und Chef des Oberkommandos der Wehrmacht in Selbstzeugniss. Werner Maser, ed. Berlin: Edition q, 1998.)

Kelley, Douglas M. 22 Cells at Nuremberg; a Psychiatrist Examines the Nazi Criminals. New York: Greenberg, 1947.

Kempner, Robert. Ankläger einer Epoche; Lebenserinnerungen; in Zusammenarbeit mit Jörg Friedrich. Berlin: Ulstein, 1983.

_______. Das Dritte Reich im Kreuzverhör; Aus den unveröffentlichten Vernehmungsprotokollen des Anklägers Robert M. W. Kempner. Originally published 1969. Düsseldorf: Droste, 1980.

King, Henry T., Jr. The Two Worlds of Albert Speer – Reflections of a Nuremberg Prosecutor. Lanham, Md.: University Press of America, Inc., 1997.

Kranzbühler, Otto. Rückblick auf Nürnberg. Hamburg: Zeit-Verlag E. Schmidt, 1949.

Lippe, Victor Freiherr von der. Nürnberger Tagebuchnotizen, November 1945 bis Oktober 1946. Frankfurt am Main: Verlag Fritz Knapp, 1951.

Martin, Roy A. Inside Nurnberg: Military Justice for Nazi War Criminals. Shippensburg, Pennsylvania: White Mane Books, 2000.

Meltzer, Bernard D. Remembering Nuremberg. Chicago: Occasional Papers (#34) from the Law School, University of Chicago, 1995.

Neave, Airey. Nuremberg: A Personal Record of the Trial of the Major Nazi War Criminals in 1945-6. London: Hodder and Stoughton, 1978. (US edition entitled: On Trial at Nuremberg. Boston: Little, Brown, 1979.)

Papen, Franz von. Memoirs. Trans. by Brian Connell. London: Andre Deutsch, 1952.

Polevoi, Boris. The Final Reckoning: Nuremberg Diaries. Trans. from the Russian. Moscow: Progress Publisher, 1978.

Poltorak, Arkadii Iosifovich. The Retribution: Notes of an Eye-Witness of the Nuremburg Trial. Trans. from the Russian. Moscow: Novosti Press Agency Publishing House, 1976.

Raeder, Erich. My Life. Trans. by Henry W. Drexel. Annapolis: U S Naval Institute, 1960.

Ribbentrop, Joachim von. The Ribbentrop Memoirs. Trans. by Oliver Watson. London: Weidenfeld and Nicolson, 1954.

Schacht, Hjalmar. Account Settled. Trans. by Edward Fitzgerald. London: Weidenfeld and Nicolson, 1949.

_______. My First Seventy-Six Years; The Autobiography of Hjalmar Schacht. Trans. by Diana Pyke. London: Alan Wingate, 1955. (U. S. edition entitled: Confessions of The Old Wizard: The Autobiography of Hjalmar Horace Greeley Schacht. Boston: Houghton Mifflin, 1956.)

Schellenberg, Walter. The Schellenberg Memoris. Louis Hagen, ed. London: Andre Deutsch, 1956.

Schirach, Baldur von. Ich Glaubte an Hitler. Hamburg: Mosaik Verlag, 1967.

Seidl, Alfred. Der Fall Rudolf Hess: Dokumentation des Verteidiges. 3d rev. ed. München: Universitas Verlag, 1988.

Shawcross, Hartley. Life Sentence: The Memoirs of Lord Shawcross. London: Constable, 1995.

Speer, Albert. Infiltration. Trans. by Joachim Neugroschel. New York: Macmillan, 1981.
_______. Inside the Third Reich: Memoirs by Albert Speer. Trans. by Richard and Clara Winston. New York: Macmillan, 1970.
_______. Spandau. The Secret Diaries. Trans. by Richard and Clara Winston. New York: The Macmillan Company, 1976.
Sprecher, Drexel A. Inside the Nuremberg Trial: A Prosecutor's Comprehensive Account. 2 vol. Lanham, Md.: University Press of America, 1999.
Storey, Robert G. The Final Judgment? Pearl Harbor to Nuremberg. San Antonio: The Naylor Company, 1968.
Taylor, Telford. The Anatomy of the Nuremberg Trial – A Personal Memoir. New York: Alfred A. Knopf, 1992.
_______. Nuremberg Trials: War Crimes and International Law. New York: Carnegie Endowment for International Peace, 1949.
Tilles, Stanley and Jeffrey Denhart. By the Neck until Dead: The Gallows of Nuremberg. Bedford, Indiana: JoNa Books, 1999.

SECONDARY SOURCES

Alexander, Charles W., and Anne Keeshan. Justice at Nuernberg: A Pictorial Record of the Trial of War Criminals by the International Tribunal at Nuernberg, Germany, 1945-46. Photographed by Charles W. Alexander, director of photography for the trials. Text by Anne Keeshan. Chicago: Marvel Press, 1946.
Apih, Elio. "Tre documenti sulla politica nazista nel litorale adriatico," Movimento di Liberazione in Italia XXXIV (1972): 37-76.
Appleman, John Alan. Military Tribunals and International Crimes. Westport, Conn.: Greenwood Press, 1971 (reprint of 1954 Bobbs-Merrill publication).
Bardens, Dennis. Lord Justice Birkett. London: Hale, 1962.
Benton, Wilbourn E. and Grimm, Georg. Nuremberg: German Views of the War Trials. Dallas: Southern Methodist University Press, 1955.
Bernstein, Victor H. Final Judgment: The Story of Nuremberg. New York: Bonnie and Gaer, 1947.
Black, Peter R. Ernst Kaltenbrunner: Ideological Soldier of the Third Reich. Princeton, New Jersey: Princeton University Press, 1984.
Bloch, M. Ribbentrop. London: Bantam Press, 1992.
Bosch, William J. Judgment on Nuremberg: American Attitudes toward the Major German War-Crime Trials. Chapel Hill: University of North Carolina Press, 1970.
Bytwerk, Randall L. Julius Streicher. New York: Dorset Press, 1988.

Clay, Lucius, D. Decision in Germany. New York: Doubleday and Company, Inc., 1950.

Conot, Robert E. Justice at Nuremberg. New York: Harper and Row, 1983.

Cooper, Robert W. The Nuremberg Trial. New York: Penguin Books, 1947.

Cotler, Irwin, ed. Nuremberg 40 Years Later: The Struggle Against Injustice in Our Time. Montreal: McGill-Queen's University Press, 1995.

Cyprian, Tadeusz and Sawicki, Jerzy. Nuremberg in Retrospect: People and Issues of the Trial. Warsaw: Western Press Agency, 1967.

Davidson, Eugene, ed. The Trial of the Germans: An Account of the Twenty-two Defendants before the International Military Tribunal at Nuremberg. Columbia, Missouri: University of Missouri Press, 1997. (Originally New York: Macmillan, 1966.

Elste, Alfred; Koschat, Michael; and Filipič, Hansi. NS-Österreich auf der Anklagebank; Anatomie eines politischen Schauprozesses im kommunistischen Slowenien. Klagenfurt: Hermagoras Verlag, 2000.

Fishman, Jack. Spandau. Rev. and updated ed. London: Grafton, 1989. (Originally published as Long Knives and Short Memories: The Lives and the Crimes of the Seven Nazis Tried at Nuremberg. London: Souvenir, 1986.)

Gaiba, F. The Origins of Simultaneous Interpretation: The Nuremberg Trial Ottawa: University of Ottawa Press, 1998.

Gallagher, Richard. Nuremberg: The Third Reich on Trial. New York: Avon Books, 1961.

Gerhart, Eugene C. America's Advocate: Robert H. Jackson. Indianapolis: Bobbs-Merrill, 1958.

_______. Robert H. Jackson: Country Lawyer, Supreme Court Justice, America's Advocate. New York: William S. Hein & Company, 2003.

Ginsburgs, George. Moscow's Road to Nuremberg: The Soviet Background to the Trial. Leiden: Brill Academic Publishers, 1996.

Ginsburgs, George and V.N. Kudriavtsev, eds. The Nuremberg Trial and International Law. Boston: Martinus Nijhoff Publishers, 1990.

Hanisch, Ernst. Nationalsozialistische Herrschaft in der Provinz Salzburg im Dritten Reich. Salzburg: Landespressebüro, 1983.

Heineman, J. L. Hitler's First Foreign Minister: Constantin von Neurath, Diplomat and Statesman. Berkeley: University of California Press, 1979.

Heydecker, Joe and Johannes Leeb. The Nuremberg Trial; A History of Nazi Germany as Revealed Through the Testimony at Nuremberg. Trans. and edited by R. A. Downie. Westport, Conn.: Greenwood Press, 1975. (The German edition has been revised as Der Nürnberg Prozess: Neue Dokumente, Erkenntnisse, und Analysen. Köln: Kiepenheuer & Witsch, 1985.

Höffkes, Karl. Hitlers politische Generale; Die Gauleiter des Dritten Reichs. Tübingen: Grabert Verlag, 1987.

Hutton, Joseph Bernard. Hess: The Man and His Mission. London: David Bruce & Watson, Ltd., 1970.
Hyde, H. Montgomery. Norman Birkett: The Life of Lord Birkett of Ulverston. Harmondsworth: Penguin, 1989.
Irving, David. Göring: A Biography. New York: Morrow, 1989.
_______. Nuremberg; The Last Battle. London: Focal Point, 1997.
Kahn, Leo. Nuremberg Trials. New York: Ballantine, 1972.
Knieriem, August von. The Nuremberg Trials. Chicago: Henry Regnery, 1959.
Kochavi, A. Prelude to Nuremberg: Allied War Crimes Policy and the Quest for Punishment. Chapel Hill: University of North Carolina Press, 1998.
Lewis, Anthony. "Bush and the Lesser Evil." New York Review of Books 51.9 (27 May 2003).
Levy, Albert G. D. "The Laws and Procedure of War Crimes Trials." The American Political Science Review XXXVII (December 1943), 1054.
Lo sterminio mancato: La dominazione nazista nel Veneto orientale 1943-1945. Ed. Pier Arrigo Carnier. Milano: Mursia, 1982.
Mann, Abby. Judgment at Nuremberg. New York: New American Library, 1961.
Manvell, Roger and Fraenkel, Heinrich. Hess, A Biography. London: MacGibbon and Kee, 1971.
Maser, Werner. Nuremberg: A Nation on Trial. Trans. by Richard Barry. London: Allen Lane, 1979.
Mendelsohn, John. Trial by Document: The Use of Seized Records in the United States Proceedings at Nürnberg. New York: Garland Pub, 1988.
Miale, Florence R. and Michael Selzer. The Nuremberg Mind: The Psychology of the Nazi Leaders. New York: Quadrangle, 1975.
Neliba, Günter. Wilhelm Frick: Der Legalist des Unrechtsstaates: Eine politische Biographie. Paderborn: Schöningh, 1992.
Neumann, H. J. Arthur Seyss-Inquart. Vienna: Verlag Styria, 1970.
Overy, Richard J. Goering: 'the Iron Man'. London: Routledge & Kegan Paul, 1984.
Padfield, Peter. Dönitz, The Last Führer: Portrait of a Nazi Leader. London: Gollancz, 1984.
_______. Hess: The Führer's Disciple. London: Cassell, 2001.
Pauley, Bruce. Hitler and the Forgotten Nazis; A History of Austrian National Socialism. Chapel Hill: University of North Carolina Press, 1981.
Persico, Joseph E. Nuremberg: Infamy on Trial. New York: Viking, 1994.
Preradovic, Nikolaus von. Österreichs Höhere SS-Führer. Berg am See: Kurt Vowinchel-Verlag, 1987.
Scheurig, B. Alfred Jodl: Gehorsam und Verhängnis. Biographie. Berlin: Propyläen, 1991.
Schmidt, M. Albert Speer: The End of a Myth. New York: St. Martin's Press, 1984.

Schwarzwäller, Wulf. Rudolf Hess: The Last Nazi. Bethesda, Md.: National Press, Inc., 1988.

Sereny, Gitta. Albert Speer: His Battle with Truth. New York: Knopf, 1995.

Shirer, William L. The Rise and Fall of the Third Reich. New York: Simon and Schuster, 1960.

Simpson, Amos P. Hjalmar Schacht in Perspective. The Hague: Mouton, 1969.

Smith, Bradley F. Reaching Judgment at Nuremberg. New York: Basic Books, 1977.

_______. The Road to Nuremberg. New York: Basic Books, 1981.

Swearingen, Ben E. The Mystery of Hermann Goering's Suicide. New York: Harcourt Brace Jovanovich, 1985.

Thompson, H.K., Jr., and Henry Strutz, eds. Doenitz at Nuremberg, A Re-appraisal: War Crimes and the Military Professional. New York: Amber Publishing Corporation, 1976.

Tusa, Ann, and Tusa, John. The Nuremberg Trial. Birmingham, Alabama: Notable Trials Library, 1990. (Reprint; originally New York: Atheneum, 1984.)

Vat, Dan van der. The Good Nazi – The Life and Lies of Albert Speer. Boston: Houghton Mifflin Company, 1997.

Walzl, August. Kärnten 1945. Klagenfurt: Universitätsverlag Carinthia, 1985.

Weitz, John. Hitler's Banker: Hjalmar Horace Greeley Schacht. Boston: Little, Brown, and Company, 1997.

_______. Joachim von Ribbentrop: Hitler's Diplomat. London: Weidenfeld and Nicholson, 1992. (U.S. edition as Hitler's Diplomat: The Life and Times of Joachim von Ribbentrop.)

West, Rebecca. A Train of Powder. London: Virago, 1984. (Originally published London: Macmillan, 1955.)

Williams, Maurice. "Delusions of Grandeur: The Austrian National Socialists." Canadian Journal of History XIV (Dec. 1979): 417-436.

_______. "Friedrich Rainer e Odilo Globocnik. L'amicizia insolita ed I ruoli sinistri di due nazisti tipici." Qualestoria (Trieste) XXV (1997): 141-175.

_______. "Friedrich Rainer, National Socialism, and Postwar Europe: The Historical World of an Austrian Nazi. Austrian History Yearbook XXX (1999): 103-126.

_______. Gau, Volk, and Reich: Friedrich Rainer and the Paradox of Austrian National Socialism. Klagenfurt, Austria: Verlag des Geschichtsvereines für Kärnten, 2005. (German edition: Gau, Volk, und Reich; Friedrich Rainer und der österreichische Nationalsozialismus; Eine politische Biographie nach Selbstzeugnissen. Klagenfurt, Austria: Verlag des Geschichtsvereines für Kärnten, 2005.)

_______. "The Nazis, German Nationalism, and Ethnic Diversity: The Adriatic Coastland under Friedrich Rainer." Slovene Studies XVII, 1-2 (1995; published August 1998): 3-23.

Woetzel, Robert K. The Nuremberg Trials in International Law, with a Postlude on the Eichmann Case. 2d edition. New York: Praeger, 1962.

Zillmer, Eric A. et al. The Quest for the Nazi Personality: A Psychological Investigation of Nazi War Criminals. Hillsdale, N.J.: Lawrence Erlbaum, 1995.

INDEX